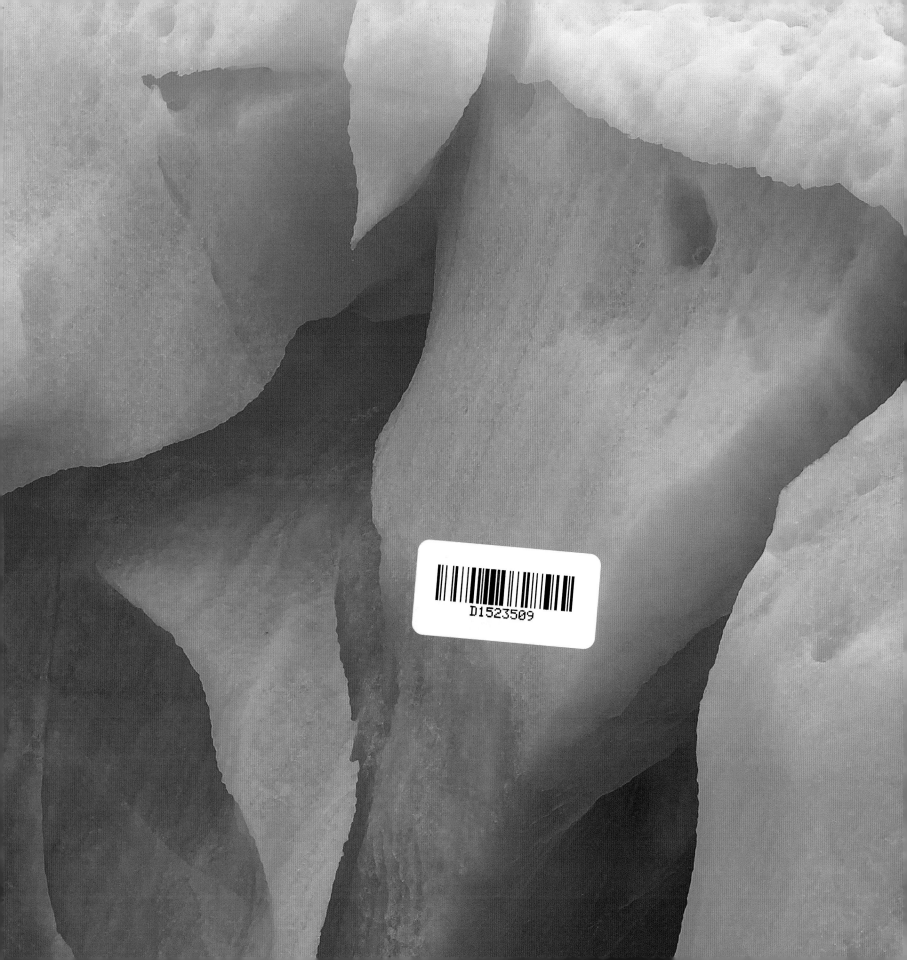

Dear Gregory

Happy Father's Day 2022.

With all our love,

Mom + Dad

The Science of Hope

Wiebke Finkler, PhD, is a creative marketing researcher, filmmaker and science communicator. With a background in marine biology, Wiebke has a special interest in how filmmaking combined with community-based social marketing can be used as a tool for human–wildlife management, sustainable development, conservation, and social good. Wiebke is currently a lecturer in the Department of Marketing, University of Otago, New Zealand.

Scott Davis is a wildlife researcher, international photography expedition leader and professional assignment photographer specializing in wildlife, travel, documentary and editorial imagery. Originally trained as a wildlife and marine biologist, Scott's research, photo assignments and expeditions have repeatedly taken him to the far remote corners of the globe and all seven continents.

The Science of Hope

EYE TO EYE WITH OUR WORLD'S WILDLIFE

DR WIEBKE FINKLER AND SCOTT DAVIS

'Only if we understand, will we care.
Only if we care, will we help.
Only if we help, shall all be saved.'

Jane Goodall

To my children Lewis, Milos and Eligh.
Dream big, fly high and always move to your own rhythm.

Hope, charisma and childhood backyards *9*

1 Whales *14*

2 Penguins *22*

3 Seals and sea lions *30*

4 Bears *39*

5 Sea Otters *48*

6 Great White Sharks *54*

7 Big Cats *65*

8 Elephants *74*

9 Giraffes *84*

10 Kangaroos *90*

11 Koalas *98*

12 Whale Sharks *106*

13 Kākā *117*

14 Monarch Butterflies *124*

15 Great Apes *135*

16 Wildlife selfies and sustainable tourism *146*

A hopeful ending *152*

Credits *156*

Index *157*

Acknowledgements *160*

Mystical ancient forest. Tararua
Range Forest, New Zealand.

Hope, charisma and childhood backyards

I have to start with a confession: I love life. Despite all of the conflicts, crises and environmental problems facing humanity, to me life is full of magic and beauty. I remain a complete and utter life-addict who gets her daily highs out of the small things in life.

As a young girl I spent my days having adventures in the forest. Growing up in a tiny village in Germany, my backyard introduced me to the magic of the natural world. I still remember lying in the grass observing birds of prey circling above me and being absorbed in a cross-species dialogue of sorts. I was mesmerized observing the dramas of everyday life: ladybirds conquering grassy peaks, ants soldiering through their macro-worlds and trees calling me to join them in the shelter of their tops. Life is such a mystery and adventure even if, at times, it seems too much to comprehend while trying to hold on for the ride. My hope is that I can play a small but positive role in the great theatre of life, and that once the final curtain closes on me, my children's world will be just that little bit better for it. We all need hope. It is such a small word

and yet it is so large in its implications; I believe that hope is as vital to our brains as the oxygen we breathe.

Hope, however, is not simply an emotion. It is the belief that our future can be better than the present — and that we can play a role in making it so. There is, it turns out, a long-established and measured science of hope. Hope Theory emerged largely through the work of C.R. Snyder in the 1990s, who noted that much of human behaviour was goal directed. Hope Theory refers to our ability to develop pathways (waypower) or mental strategies that will help us achieve our goals and apply our agency (willpower) to these pathways. It comes down to our choices, our goal setting, and our goal achievement before, during and after adversity.

Hope does not appear to relate to IQ or to income — it is a resource available to us all for creating or enhancing resilience. Research shows that a feeling of hopefulness changes our brains: when we feel hopeful, we are rewarded with chemicals (endorphins and enkephalins) that block pain and fast-track healing. Hope

buffers stress and adversity, it predicts important outcomes, and it can be learnt and sustained. Through hope, we overcome hurdles and move to a place of recovery. So what happens if we apply this idea to our planet and environment? In scientific terms, hope and recovery are correlated. The science of hope is pivotal to the conservation of species around the world, because hope can be a catalyst for action. This is especially relevant for environmental and conservation projects.

While most of us like to think of ourselves as egalitarian, it is clear that when it comes to animals, we often consider some species to be 'more equal than others'. Conservation programs around the world rely on the fact that the public and policymakers find some species more charismatic than others. In conservation biology, these are known as flagship species and they are used as ambassadors for particular campaigns or environmental causes. Typically, such flagship species are animals that are iconic or cute and have a unique appeal, such as Polar Bears, Giant Pandas and whales.

'There is no use talking about the problem,
unless you talk about the solution.'

Attributed to Betty Williams (Peace Activist)

The appeal of charismatic species is generated by several factors, including their looks, behaviour and overall relatability. Cuteness is a subjective term for attractiveness, but it has its basis in science. The German Nobel Prize winner and ethologist, Konrad Lorenz, proposed the concept of 'baby schema' *(Kindchenschema)*: a set of facial and body features that make a creature appear 'cute', and release in others the motivation to care for it, which helps its survival. Baby schema traits include a disproportionately large round face, big eyes situated just below the midline of the face, chubby cheeks, a large forehead, a round body and soft exterior. In humans, such a bundle of attributes will essentially bring out the mothering instincts in those observing it because of the feeling of euphoria it triggers. However, baby schema is not limited to human babies — anything with baby schema traits, including animals, will also be considered cute.

This book, then, is a compendium of charismatic creatures that enjoy international popularity and are utilized to focus society's attention on conservation. People tend to protect and restore the natural world when they feel connected with nature. These cute and charismatic animals evoke such connections, and not just for themselves — they can create a halo effect that connects us to other animals, plants and places too. In essence, they can re-awaken the fascination and concern for nature often evident in early childhood experiences. Such connection can invoke responsibility, and such responsibility can lead to action. For conservation. For saving the planet. And this is what gives me hope!

Throughout this book, I'll be sharing with you not just my hopes, but the stories and dreams of researchers who have devoted their lives to understanding these flagship species and to promoting a message of hope for our world. And we can start now, even in our very own backyards.

**Childhood memories. Ladybird
in Pannonhalma, Hungary.**

CASE STUDY

The backyards of urban New Zealand

Yolanda Van Heezik,
Urban Ecologist

Opposite: Looking up. Forest in Felton, California, USA.

There is mounting evidence that spending time in nature is good for human health. In fact, opportunities for children to connect with nature are important for the preservation of the biosphere. According to the Biophilia Theory humans have an inborn tendency to affiliate with nature. Richard Louv, in his book *Last Child in the Woods*, suggests that a disconnect between children and nature results in 'nature deficit disorder'. When children spend less time out in nature, they suffer more from problems such as difficulty concentrating, high stress levels and poor physical health. Our study looked at how and where children interact with nature in their neighbourhoods, when moving independently or with other children. The children (aged nine to eleven years old) recorded the places they travelled and spent time on an interactive map. We were able to define the biodiversity value of different urban habitats by developing a system for ranking them based upon the features and numbers of the plants and animals that could be easily seen. We were then able to determine whether children chose to spend time in places that were more biodiverse, as well as measuring their 'home range' sizes (the area they moved through in the neighbourhood) and learnt about the various factors that constrained their movements.

WHY DO YOU DO WHAT YOU DO?

I am an urban ecologist and conservation biologist. My urban research started in about 2005 with a focus on the wildlife that occupies urban landscapes, but moved towards a more socio-ecological focus. When working in urban areas, it is inevitable that people become a main focus if the purpose of your research is to provide information to support the conservation and restoration of biodiversity. Our study on backyard biodiversity brought this home to me. Urban residents make the decisions that determine how their gardens are managed, and their votes determine the decisions that councils make when designing and managing green spaces and species. People are also often unknowing beneficiaries of the nature that surrounds them. Socio-ecological research on urban biodiversity hopefully provides insights that allow us to design living environments that are good for both the health of humans and the ecosystem.

WHAT DO YOU THINK IS THE PUBLIC APPEAL OF YOUR ANIMAL?

That's easy. Our study animals in this case were children, and most people have a natural affiliation towards children, particularly their own!

WHAT HAVE BEEN YOUR BIGGEST LESSONS LEARNT?

Even though all children had at least one green space within their immediate neighbourhood, various constraints (mostly social) meant that only two-thirds of children actually accessed a green space. Most children did not spend time in the most biodiverse spaces within their home ranges. We think gardens could be playing an important role in supporting children's connection to nature. Gardens don't hold wild or pristine nature, but they can have quite high biodiversity. Importantly, they were often the most biodiverse habitat that children did spend time in. So we think that children are innately biophilic, but expression of biophilia is being restricted due to lifestyle factors, with gardens being the safest and easiest place for children to interact within nature.

WHAT ARE YOUR 'STRATEGIES OF HOPE' FOR CONSERVATION?

Our research suggests we need a stronger focus on children's social environments, such as encouraging more independent mobility: some children in the study were not allowed to leave their backyard without adult supervision. Social factors also played an important role in determining children's nature knowledge. More deprived neighbourhoods supported less biodiversity in their private spaces, indicating the importance of the provision of biodiverse public spaces close to homes in such areas. Programs that incentivise householders to create more biodiverse private spaces would have the largest impact on the amount of nature children encounter.

WHAT ARE YOUR HOPES FOR THE FUTURE?

Cities designed to provide liveable habitats for more than just one species (i.e. more than just humans). Living environments where people in all parts of a city can experience meaningful encounters with wildlife as part of their regular day-to-day activities.

Whales

Whales put the *mega* into charismatic megafauna. They are the largest living things that have ever existed upon Earth. Yet not too long ago we hunted them to near extinction. Now, however, we are at risk of loving them to death.

We are intrigued by whales: they are mammals like us, yet they appear otherworldly, floating through the oceans like gargantuan submarines. There are two basic types: toothed whales and baleen whales. Most of the world's 90 different whale species are toothed whales, including one of the most charismatic of all, the **Killer Whale** or **Orca** which, in fact, is the largest member of the dolphin family. They have teeth and hunt their prey using echolocation, although Killer Whales are especially famous for nearly beaching themselves in order to snatch unsuspecting seals and penguins from the surf close to shore.

Baleen whales, by comparison, do not use echolocation and feed instead by using baleen, skin-like plates that hang down from their upper jaws and are used to filter their prey from the seawater.

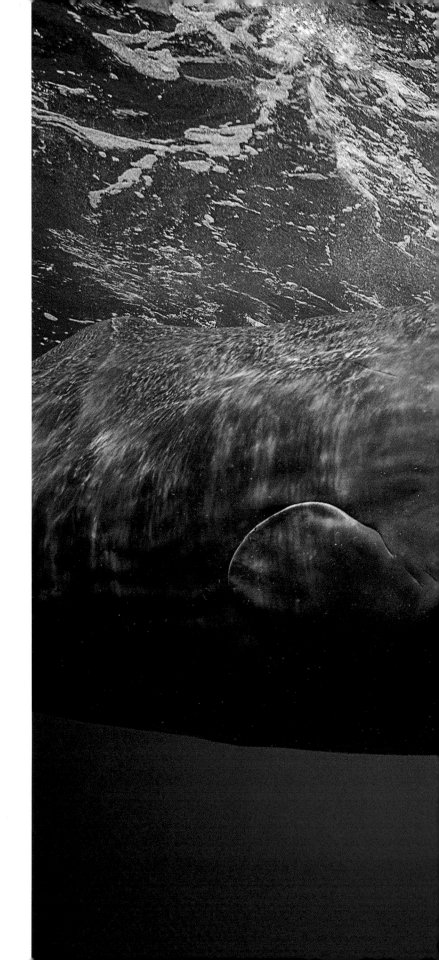

Sperm Whale, Dominica. An inquisitive adolescent Sperm Whale comes in for a closer inspection.

Left: Feeding Humpback Whale displaying baleen plates for filtering zooplankton in the inshore waters of Antarctica.

Opposite: Female Killer Whale breaching off the coast of Monterey Bay, California, USA.

They have two blowholes on top of their heads, compared to only one for toothed whales.

The most obvious thing that attracts us to whales is that they are undeniably big. No other creature, even in the Age of the Dinosaurs, has ever got close to the size of a **Blue Whale**, which can be over 30 metres (98 feet) in length and weigh more than 170 tonnes. The **Sperm Whale** is the largest of the toothed whales and is infamous for eating Giant Squid, for which they can dive to depths of over 2000 metres (6561 feet) and stay down, holding their breaths, for up to 90 minutes. The round scars and marks that can be found on a Sperm Whale's head come courtesy of confrontations with Giant Squid,

which latch onto the whale in an attempt to avoid being eaten.

Another thing that makes whales irresistible to us is their obvious intelligence. They communicate with each other using an extremely intricate system of sounds and displays. The songs of **Humpback Whales** are some of the most complex calls in the animal kingdom, and their 'vocabulary' of different sounds may even exceed our own. Each pod of whales has its own dialect, which helps distinguish the whales in their own pod from whales of another pod. Male Humpbacks court females with songs that can last for hours.

And whales don't just 'talk' to each other.

They engage in amazing visual displays too, slapping their tails and flippers on the surface of the sea and, most spectacularly of all, breaching, when they somehow propel their giant bodies completely out of the water and flop down on the surface with a loud splash. It is this, in particular, that has made them the darlings of the wildlife tourism industry, which has been both the whales' blessing and their curse. We stopped hunting them with harpoons and now we pursue them with cameras instead. But, just as the likes of the Humpback Whales are making a remarkable comeback after being driven almost to extinction for their meat, oil, bone and baleen, our desire to get close to them, to photograph them breaching and to marvel at their great size is risking harming them yet again.

Whale watching can have serious negative impacts on populations of whales due to proximity and speed of boats, boat crowding, underwater noise pollution and disturbance of their important behaviours such as sleeping, feeding, resting and nursing their young. Yet responsible whale watching, which should occur at an appropriately respectful distance from the

whales, has the potential to benefit whales and the ecology of the oceans themselves by raising environmental awareness and inducing pro-environmental behavioural change in us.

Anyone who watches these charismatic creatures cannot help but become an ambassador for them and their wellbeing. Citizen science projects that engage the public in monitoring the whales are another way to turn a potential negative into a positive outcome for them. For example, the Happy Whale initiative uses the collective power of photographs taken by whale watchers to identify whales from the individual markings on their flippers and tail flukes and, thereby, plot such things as their movements, survival and breeding success.

Our choice is a simple one: choose responsible whale-watching tour operators who know how best to behave around these majestic animals to avoid harm. This is the only way to ensure these gentle giants are not over-exploited yet again for our own benefit and that we will always have them around to elicit our feelings of awe.

Above: Two worlds of above and below water. Humpback Whale with calf swimming away in the offshore waters of the Dominican Republic.

Opposite: Humpback Whale with her calf, Kingdom of Tonga.

CASE STUDY

Whales of Guerrero

Katherina Audley, Marine
Educator/Conservationist

My organization, the Whales
of Guerrero, uses science to
connect people with nature
and kickstart conservation.
Our approach is to cultivate
local leadership through citizen
science with Humpback Whales.
We are working to galvanize
a group of leaders to develop
community-designed marine
management and protection
plans that work for everyone.

Curious Humpback Whale
calf, Kingdom of Tonga.

WHY DO YOU DO WHAT YOU DO?

I was struck by whale fever in the late 1990s when I realized that there are these animals — the largest animals that have ever lived — swimming around in the ocean right in front of us. And they are incredibly smart and complex: they have distinct cultures, languages, familial relationships and they experience life on Earth in a way we can't comprehend. They are mostly acoustic animals and it is nothing to them to travel the world's oceans, passing by canyons and creatures we know nothing about. When you go eye to eye with a whale and it takes you in, that's as close as I can imagine to interacting with an alien.

WHAT DO YOU THINK IS THE PUBLIC APPEAL OF YOUR ANIMAL?

Humpback Whales in particular are very flamboyant and funny. They breach, tail-lob and fin-slap more than the other whales. The males sing long, complex songs and the calves are curious and goofy. What's not to love?

WHAT HAVE BEEN YOUR BIGGEST LESSONS LEARNT?

It's not difficult for me to be committed to supporting a healthy ocean and community of environmental stewards in and of itself. However, it is at times a challenge to keep my energy up given the continual ongoing and new factors getting lobbed our way, both internally and externally, and the amount of time and energy it takes to secure funds to continue. Continuing on despite setbacks can require a kind of optimism that feels delusional at times.

WHAT ARE YOUR 'STRATEGIES OF HOPE' FOR CONSERVATION?

There are thousands of species to fall in love with and so many opportunities to engage local communities with nature — it doesn't have to be just about whales. My message is that a few committed people really can save the world, one corner at a time.

WHAT ARE YOUR HOPES FOR THE FUTURE?

I dream of a world where inspired and empowered local leaders are guiding their communities in a way that takes the entire surrounding ecology's wellbeing into consideration with every decision they make. My greatest hope is that we are able to reverse the disconnection from nature and the degradation we have created, so we can continue to enjoy and share life on Earth with all of the amazing animals and plants that are alive today.

Below: Whales of Guerrero educational community program.

Penguins

Chapter co-written with Lloyd Spencer Davis

Penguins are some of the world's best-loved birds, able to warm our hearts even at the coldest temperatures. Their distinctive looks and comedic character mean that they are instantly recognizable; a firmly established part of popular culture. Penguins — especially baby Emperor Penguins — have the 'cute' factor. They are birds, but they stand upright and walk like us. We cannot help but be fascinated by the funny way penguins waddle and their amazing lifestyles.

There are eighteen species of penguins, all of which are found in the Southern Hemisphere. As flightless birds, the wings of penguins have been modified to form flippers that help them to swim and dive deep in the water. In a way, they fly through water. The largest species, the **Emperor Penguin**, is able to stay underwater for more than 27 minutes and reach depths of over 560 metres (1837 feet), where they feed on fish and squid. Other penguins eat mainly krill, a shrimp-like crustacean found in vast swarms.

While they give the impression of having a better dress sense than us, the tuxedo-like appearance of penguins actually serves a very important purpose

On an unseasonably warm day in Antarctica, Emperor Penguin chicks lay their torsos flat on the snow in an effort to cool down.

Emperor Penguin chick soliciting a meal from its parent. Antarctica.

by providing a form of camouflage known as countershading. From above, their black backs blend into the murky depths of the ocean; from below, their white bellies are hidden against the bright surface. This way, even in the open ocean, they can sneak up on prey and remain hard to see for their predators.

The Emperor Penguin weighs in at more than 35 kilograms (77 pounds) and stands around 1.2 metres (4 feet) tall. Incredibly, it breeds in the coldest conditions endured by any bird — during the Antarctic winter, when temperatures can reach -40°C (-40°F) and wind speeds can be over 145 kilometres per hour (90 miles per hour). To help them survive in this environment, Emperor Penguins have the highest feather density of any bird: fifteen feathers per square centimetre (100 feathers per square inch), which traps warm air next to their skin. Male Emperor Penguins use their feet as a nest, incubating a single egg on top of their feet, which they cover with their bellies to keep the egg warm. **King Penguins**, the second-largest penguin species, can form large colonies when they come ashore during the mating season. These colourful birds look very different to their brown down-covered chicks, which look more like teddy bears than penguins. The chicks take over one year to develop and they can be left alone for months at a time while their parents travel hundreds, or even thousands, of miles to get food.

While most penguins nest in colonies, **Yellow-eyed Penguins** live in isolated pairs and dwell on the forest floors and grassy coastlines of New Zealand. The only penguin species with yellow eyes, they have become a flagship species for nature-based tourism in New Zealand. **Little Penguins** are the smallest penguins, standing just over 30 centimetres (1 foot) high and tipping the scales at around 1 kilogram (2 pounds). They are found in New Zealand and Australia where, especially at Phillip Island, they have become a major tourist attraction. This appeal of penguins is also evidenced at other places where penguins live in close proximity to humans and have become the basis of major tourism industries, such as the **African Penguin** in South Africa, the **Magellanic Penguin** in Argentina, the **Humboldt Penguin** in Peru and Chile, and the **Galápagos Penguin** in the Galápagos Islands.

Above: Yellow-Eyed Penguin resting on Otago Peninsula, New Zealand.

Left: King Penguin chicks form groups called creches. Typically, any adult that passes through will be solicited for food regardless of parentage. South Georgia Island.

King Penguins returning from
the sea. South Georgia Island.

Left: Emperor Penguin grooming chick, Antarctica.

Below: King Penguins assessing the dangers before heading back out to sea. Falkland Islands.

It is just as well, because it is the cute appeal of penguins that might ultimately save them: two-thirds of penguin species are declining at an alarming rate and in almost every case where the causes can be identified, the culprits are us. We harvest their eggs and guano, take the fish and krill they eat, introduce mammalian predators to their breeding areas, destroy their habitats, pollute their waters, and change the ecology of the oceans through global warming.
Perhaps when we see such endearing creatures suffering at our own hands, we might change our ways!

King and Rockhopper penguins in the Falklands

Klemens Pütz, Marine Zoologist

For 30 years I have been studying the feeding ecology and winter dispersal of penguins, with a particular focus on King and Southern Rockhopper Penguins. I co-founded the Antarctic Research Trust (ART), a charity that conducts scientific research to provide baseline data for conservation, and have been acting as scientific director since. ART has purchased five islands in the Falkland archipelago with the ultimate goal of establishing a wildlife sanctuary in the Southwest Atlantic. I attach small data loggers or transmitters that record the penguins' feeding location, diving behaviour and swimming speed. Improved knowledge about how penguins function in their environment can be used to apply appropriate conservation measures so as to reverse the population decline apparent in many species.

Klemens Pütz (left) deploying a tag on a Rockhopper Penguin in the Falkland Islands.

Rockhopper Penguins in breeding colony in the Falkland Islands.

WHY DO YOU DO WHAT YOU DO?

During my childhood, I had a great affection for nature and, rather than doing my homework, I was always out and about. Even after 30 years of working in remote environments, I thoroughly enjoy it. I see it as a little bit like soul-washing, having to restrict your way of living to that which is absolutely necessary for personal wellbeing and survival. Ultimately, it is very rewarding to be able to improve, even on a small scale, the living conditions of penguins.

When finishing my studies in biology, I got to spend a summer in Antarctica with Emperor Penguins. The beauty and isolation of Antarctica struck me immediately, only to be topped by encountering the penguins. I fell in love with these iconic creatures, which, later on, expanded to other penguin species residing further north. My fascination with penguins has increased the more I learn about them, and so has my desire to protect these birds in a worsening environment so that, I hope, my grandchildren will still have the chance to encounter penguins the way I did.

Rockhopper Penguin with distinctive yellow crest.

WHAT DO YOU THINK IS THE PUBLIC APPEAL OF YOUR ANIMAL?

Penguins are recognized worldwide as a charismatic species, which is most likely linked to their human-like appearance when ashore. However, once in the water, you realize how favourably adapted they are to an aquatic lifestyle.

WHAT HAVE BEEN YOUR BIGGEST LESSONS LEARNT?

The adaptations of penguins to their aquatic lifestyle have fascinated me. Underwater, they are perfectly adapted torpedo-like projectiles. They can migrate thousands of miles to food-rich areas and navigate home with the highest precision to their nest sites.

WHAT ARE YOUR 'STRATEGIES OF HOPE' FOR CONSERVATION?

A profound knowledge of penguins will enable us to identify the major threats to them and to take appropriate action to preserve these beautiful creatures for future generations. From this, not only the penguins, but also humankind and, ultimately, the whole blue planet will benefit.

WHAT ARE YOUR HOPES FOR THE FUTURE?

I hope that the 'attractiveness' of penguins will help us to raise enough public awareness to convince political bodies to take adequate conservation measures to ensure the penguins' survival in the wild. By doing so, we would also, inevitably, improve our own environment and prevent the worst impacts of the forecasted global climate change.

CHAPTER 3

Seals and sea lions

Seals are the acrobats of the sea: twisting and turning in the water with such ease, they give little hint that they are derived from land-based ancestors that trotted about on all fours. In contrast, when out of the water they seem to amble at best, shuffle at worst, and spend a good deal of their time sleeping. And it is partly this contrasting image of the fun-filled party animal in the water paired with the insouciant slouch out of it that gives seals their charisma. That, and their big, dark, beautiful eyes.

Yet the story of any one seal is really the story of virtually all seals everywhere: once numerous and widespread, they were hunted to near extinction, became protected, and are now making a recovery. If they appear not to sweat the small stuff, perhaps it is because the world they know now is a relatively

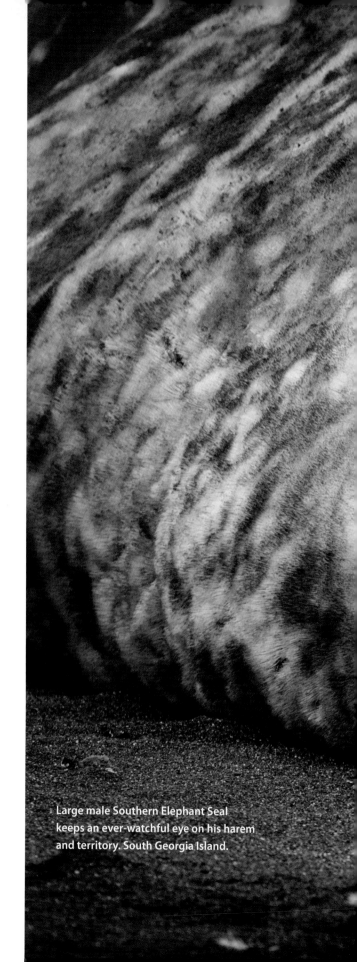

Large male Southern Elephant Seal keeps an ever-watchful eye on his harem and territory. South Georgia Island.

Right: Leopard Seal in Antarctica.

Opposite: Walrus with impressively large tusks. Svalbard, Norway.

benign place compared to their brutal past.

Seals are marine mammals that are found living throughout the world, from the polar regions to the tropics. They evolved from bear- and otter-like ancestors about 25 million years ago. In fact, a recently discovered fossil seal in Canada, known as Puijila, may well be the evolutionary link in the transition of seals from land to water: it lived in water but walked on all fours and had a long tail like an otter.

Modern seals are divided in three families. One is the Otariid or 'eared' seals, such as fur seals and sea lions. These seals have external ear flaps, walk on all four flippers when on land, and when in water propel themselves with their front flippers. In contrast, Phocid seals have no ear flaps, are unable to move their hind flippers under their bodies and so when on land move in a caterpillar motion, while in water propulsion is provided by the hind flippers. This group constitutes what is sometimes called the true seals and includes Elephant, Leopard, Harp and Weddell seals. The third family group contains the **Walrus**. In all, there are 33 species of seals.

Seals have a layer of fat under their skin called blubber, which enables these warm-blooded mammals like us to stay warm when immersed in water for long periods. Their slick fur coat is streamlined for gliding through water, and

their whiskers help them detect the vibration of their prey under water. Many seals feed on fish, but some have much more specialized diets, such as the **Crabeater Seal**, which — despite its name — eats mainly krill, and the **Leopard Seal**, which snacks on penguins and even other seals.

Seals spend much of their life in water, but they breed onshore or on sea ice. Some breed in large colonies. Others mate in the water and give birth on the ice. Seals can even sleep underwater.

Seals have 'delayed implantation', so that even though gestation is typically about nine to

ten months and mating takes place soon after the female has given birth to a pup, the new pup will not be born until a year later. Males contribute only their sperm to their offspring: all the parenting is provided by the mothers.

Elephant Seals are the heavyweight champions of the seal world, with an adult male weighing in at up to 4000 kilograms (8800 pounds) and measuring up to 6 metres (20 feet) in length! Adult females are much smaller — as little as one-tenth of the weight of the males. The males use their size and inflated snouts to compete with each other, and successful males

Left: Group of resting Elephant Seals. Falkland Islands.

Below: Large male Southern Elephant Seal with female.

Opposite: Adult Walrus surveying his surroundings in the frozen waters off Svalbard, Norway.

may have a harem of many females.

Elephant Seals can dive to depths of over 1.6 kilometres (1 mile) and hold their breath for up to two hours! Their milk is extremely rich in fats so the pups can gain weight rapidly. It is a characteristic of especially the true seals that pups grow very quickly and are weaned rapidly, often within a few weeks of being born.

Indeed, it is the vulnerable pups with their gorgeous thick pelts and big dark eyes that contribute a lot to the public appeal of seals. Images of such pups engendered public outcry in the 1980s and brought a halt to the clubbing to death of young, white-coated Harp Seal pups. Yet, even today, about half a million seals are slaughtered worldwide for their pelts, which are used largely by the fashion industry. Sometimes being charismatic just doesn't seem enough. And sometimes being charismatic seems like too much, such as when people harass you to have their photo taken with you.

CASE STUDY

Tourism with a seal of approval

Chantal Pagel, Conservation Biologist

Wildlife tourism has become incredibly popular, such as commercial swim-with programs, with animals such as seals. I want to learn why tourists want to be with seals and what their greatest challenges are when pursuing this activity. I'm particularly interested in how tourists feel about human–wildlife encounters on social media: for example, what do they think about wildlife selfies and do they take selfies of themselves in the water with the seals? I interview them about their perceptions of seals, which gives exciting insights into people's relationships with these animals.

Chantal Pagel working in the field in New Zealand.

Right: Southern Fur Seal pup. South Georgia Island.

WHY DO YOU DO WHAT YOU DO?

I started my journey in a very traditional way, by focusing on the global whale watching phenomenon. To eventually become a conservation biologist, I decided to get myself into a doctoral program. I included the New Zealand Fur Seal in my study to learn about risk perceptions and the role of social media within touristic swim activities.

WHAT DO YOU THINK IS THE PUBLIC APPEAL OF YOUR ANIMAL?

Being marine mammals already constitutes a big draw for many to get interested in seals. Most seals come with features that are appealing to people: big eyes, furry and sometimes curious; they are playful and clumsy, readily making eye contact and, therefore, are perceived as cute. Sometimes referred to as 'mermaid dogs', animal lovers draw comparisons to their pets at home and, although being highly specialized predators they're generally not perceived as a potential threat.

WHAT ARE YOUR 'STRATEGIES OF HOPE' FOR CONSERVATION?

With the rise of social media and the influence of online wildlife photography, the approach distances to wild animals have steadily decreased. People are frequently found to enter seal colonies to take up-close images (e.g. wildlife selfies) of resting animals, to throw objects or make noises to elicit a response — all to feed their social media accounts. I have learnt that educational elements about appropriate camera use can make a difference; that taking great pictures and respecting the personal space of animals are not mutually exclusive. It is also crucial to reconsider online marketing materials to mitigate expectations and undesired tourist behaviour, such as those that involve close approaches to try to copy previously seen content on social media. Empowering tourists to make better decisions when encountering seals can have a positive effect on tourist health and safety as well as the animals' welfare.

Panda Bear resting in a tree.

CHAPTER 2

Bears

Bears are a contradiction. They exude a cuteness and cuddliness that belies the likely lethality of a real bear hug. Certainly, bear cubs, like teddy bears, are irresistibly adorable with their big eyes, fluffy bodies, clumsy movements and large heads awakening our caring instincts. While there are eight different species of bears distributed across the world, there are three that pull strongest on our heart strings.

Giant Pandas really do look like large black and white teddy bears, the epitome of fluff appeal with their cartoonish big ears and slow-moving antics. This appeal has turned the panda into the poster child for environmental protection and even the logo for the World Wildlife Fund.

Pandas live in remote, mountainous regions in China. Due to their elusive existence in the wild, much of what we know about pandas comes from studying them in breeding centres

Above: Polar Bear in Svalbard, Norway.

Opposite: Fishing Grizzly Bear with salmon. Alaska.

and zoos. They are often observed eating in a relaxed sitting posture, with their back legs stretched out in front of them. But don't let their sedentary looks deceive you: they are skilled tree-climbers and efficient swimmers. Pandas have an almost insatiable appetite for bamboo and typically spend half their lives eating — or about twelve hours out of every day!

Brown Bears, or **Grizzlies**, are charismatic symbols of the wilderness. Once widespread, human settlements and hunting have eliminated most of their population. Males can tower over

3 metres (10 feet) tall when standing on hind legs and they can weigh over 770 kilograms (1700 pounds), which, should you stumble across one in the wild, is guaranteed to raise your heart rate! Grizzlies are powerful, top-of-the-food-chain predators, yet much of their diet consists of nuts, berries, fruit, leaves and roots. Although they look like lumbering giants, they have been clocked running at over 50 kilometres per hour (30 miles per hour) — faster than many horses!

Polar Bears are one of the most iconic and recognizable creatures, the symbol for

climate change. The image of a white Polar Bear, the largest land carnivore in the world, in a shrinking world of ice has become the de facto representation of global warming.

Like whales, dolphins and seals, Polar Bears are considered marine mammals, and this is because they spend most of their lives on the sea ice of the Arctic Ocean. They can swim for long distances: their large paws are specially adapted for swimming, and they use them to paddle through the water while holding their hind legs flat like a rudder. They have a thick layer of body fat and a water-repellent coat that helps insulate them from the cold. In fact, the great white bear of the north is actually not white. Their fur is translucent and only appears white because it reflects visible light — actual Polar Bear skin is jet black.

Polar Bears need sea ice to survive. They rely on it for hunting, travelling, breeding and sometimes denning. Although about half of a Polar Bear's life is spent hunting for food, which consists mainly of seals, less than 2 per cent of their hunts are successful. Polar bears have an amazing sense of smell. They can sniff out a seal on the ice from about 32 kilometres (20 miles) away. They can also use their sense of smell to locate seals under layers of packed snow. Their sense of smell is especially useful for hunting at night and during times of low visibility, which happens a lot in the Arctic.

Female Grizzly Bear with cubs in Alaska, USA.

Right: Polar Bear wandering on ice. Franz Josef Land, Russia.

Male Polar Bears weigh up to 800 kilograms (1700 pounds) — twice the size of females. Despite their huge size when they're fully grown, they start off incredibly small: about the size of a hamster. Weighing a little under 1 kilogram (around 2 pounds), Polar Bear cubs are born blind, toothless and barely covered with enough fur to insulate them from the cold. Thanks to their mother's nutritious milk, which contains approximately 31 per cent fat, the cubs grow quickly and stay with their mothers for two years.

A Polar Bear's paws are nature's ultimate snowshoe, designed for traversing the slick and shifting seascape. They are enormous, with the average paw being about 30 centimetres (12 inches) wide and covered in small bumps (called papillae) that help them to grip the ice and avoid slipping. Tufts of fur between the cushions of their paws also contribute to the paws' traction, as do their sharp, powerful claws. When the ice is very thin, the bears extend their legs far apart and lower their bodies so as to distribute their weight more evenly.

Everything about Polar Bears screams 'adapted for a life on the ice'. Hence, when the Arctic ice is disappearing as rapidly as it is, it's no wonder the future of Polar Bears looks bleak. How to stop global warming and how to save the Polar Bears are obviously really big issues but, somewhat ironically, this is where tourism can potentially help.

Left: Grizzly Bear cub — a teddy bear with claws.

CASE STUDY

Polar Bears in Churchill

Jill Bueddefeld, Social Scientist

Tourism to remote or ecologically fragile areas is often considered an effective way for people to connect with places, people and wildlife. These tourism experiences often have lofty goals: visitors will learn about environmental issues and become ambassadors for the places and wildlife they visit. My research examines nature-based tourism experiences in Churchill, Canada. Churchill, in the province of Manitoba, is known as the 'Polar Bear capital of the world' and is already experiencing visible effects of climate change.

WHY DO YOU DO WHAT YOU DO?

I grew up on a small farm on the Canadian prairies. I always saw people as a part of nature, rather than separate from it. When I moved to a city for university, I realized that not everyone had this personal relationship with nature and I felt that environmental issues were often not understood due to an urban disconnect. Climate change is a great example of this. It's a big problem that affects us all, but it feels distant. Large, charismatic megafauna can help people emotionally connect with nature and we need research that explores how this connection works.

WHAT DO YOU THINK IS THE PUBLIC APPEAL OF YOUR ANIMAL?

Polar Bears appeal to the public for a few reasons. Historically, they were portrayed as terrifying predators in National Geographic specials like *Polar Bear Alert!* So they first captured the public's interest as dangerous and exotic white bears. Then, Coca-Cola commercials featured Polar Bears and they were portrayed as cute and cuddly. In recent times, they have also become icons for climate change.

WHAT HAVE BEEN YOUR BIGGEST LESSONS LEARNT?

Just seeing Polar Bears is not necessarily effective for learning about climate change. Skilled interpretation is needed for visitors to make meaningful connections between Polar Bears, the impact that climate change is having on the species, and what people can do about this. How these narratives are crafted is extremely important. It's very easy to leave people feeling hopeless and unsure about what they can do.

Polar bears in Churchill, Canada, with tour buses in the background.

**Female Polar Bear with cub.
Svalbard, Norway.**

WHAT ARE YOUR 'STRATEGIES OF HOPE' FOR CONSERVATION?

My research demonstrates that wildlife tourism featuring charismatic megafauna, such as the Polar Bear, is a potentially effective way for visitors to learn about climate change and experience transformative behavioural change. However, there needs to be a 'strategy of hope'. This means you don't leave people with the equivalent of a cliffhanger — you can't just end at the part where climate change is impacting Polar Bears and many will not survive. You need to complete that narrative by bringing the 'what's next?' into the discussion.

It means providing visitors with a few ideas of what they can do to help. This changes the visitor experience from one that can feel overwhelming and sad, to one that is hopeful and empowering.

WHAT ARE YOUR HOPES FOR THE FUTURE?

My hope for the future is that tourism and environmental educators will think more carefully about their roles, that they will recognize that learning can be much deeper and more meaningful. Communication skills are an important part of the social science of climate change education and we need to take them much more seriously.

Sea Otters

The **Southern Sea Otter**, also known as the **California Sea Otter**, is the heaviest and yet undeniably cutest member of the weasel family, but one of the smallest marine mammals. Adult Sea Otters can weigh anywhere between 13 and 27 kilograms (30–100 pounds). They are more than just a pretty face, however, being ecosystem superheroes or, as scientists are prone to say, keystone species. A keystone species is a species that is critical to how an ecosystem functions because it has large-scale impacts on the communities in which it lives.

Along the Pacific coast of North America, Sea Otters help control the populations of sea urchins: they eat sea urchins, which graze on giant kelp. No Sea Otters, no kelp forests. Following an international ban on hunting Sea Otters, their numbers rebounded in many areas. Still, they remain classified as Endangered by the International Union for the Conservation of Nature. The problem: Sea Otters have a number of characteristics that make them an easy target for disturbance by humans.

Sea Otters eat, sleep, mate and give birth

A raft of Sea Otters.

Above: Grooming Sea Otter.

in the water, and can spend their entire lives in water without ever leaving it. They have water-repellent fur to keep them dry and warm, as well as webbed feet, and nostrils and ears that close when underwater. Sea Otter fur is the densest on Earth, with an estimated 1 million hairs per square inch! Unlike other marine mammals, they have no blubber to keep them warm. If a Sea Otter's fur becomes matted and dirty, it will have trouble trapping the air needed to insulate the animal's body from the waters in which it lives. Therefore, Sea Otters are somewhat obsessive about grooming themselves to keep their fur clean. They often float at the sea's surface, lying on their backs in a posture that suggests serene repose. Sometimes, they gather in groups called 'rafts'.

Above: Sea Otter feeding on a crab.

Below: Sea Otter mother and pup in Monterey Bay, USA.

The Sea Otter is one of the few mammal species to use a tool to help it hunt and feed. After hunting on the sea floor, a Sea Otter will return to the surface to eat. Floating on its back and using its chest as a table, the Sea Otter often uses a rock to crack open its prey — especially if it is a dinner of crab, clam, snail or mussel. They also use rocks to hammer abalone and dislodge them from the underwater surface to which they are clinging. Sea Otters have built-in pouches of loose skin under their armpits to store both the food they have gathered and the rocks they use to crack it open.

A newborn pup needs constant attention and will stay with its mother for six months until it develops the requisite survival skills. An otter pup's fur is so dense that it cannot dive underwater until it gets its adult fur. Mothers can leave their pups floating on the water's surface while they search for food, knowing they are safe from drowning. Unfortunately, what Sea Otters cannot rely on, whether an adult or pup resting on the surface, is that they are safe from us.

Southern Sea Otter

Michelle Staedler, Ecologist

Over the past 35 years I have focused my research on behaviour of the Southern Sea Otter with an emphasis on mothers and pups. By being able to identify individual females with the use of flipper tags and instrumentation, I have focused on investigating how one female rears her pup versus another female, or if male pups are cared for differently than female pups. What makes one female more successful at weaning multiple pups compared to another female in the same geographic area? Does diet play a key factor? If a Sea Otter mum teaches her pup to also specialize in snails and using tools, will this pup have a better chance at surviving to weaning age and beyond than a mum and pup with a different foraging strategy? All of these questions are ones I have focused on, with one question often just leading to another intriguing question to try to study and answer.

WHY DO YOU DO WHAT YOU DO?

I study Sea Otters simply because I enjoy observing animal behaviour; it's like detective work in some ways. Trying to figure out how, what and why an animal does what it does. It is important to learn these things with all animals, but with a species that is listed as threatened as a result of human actions (fur trade hunting in the case of the Sea Otter) it is even more important to in order to help them continue to thrive. I have always loved marine life, and patiently watched snails, hermit crabs and other invertebrates in tide pools. When I moved from the Atlantic to the Pacific coast of United States as an undergraduate, the Sea Otter was a new and unique species for me to observe, and easy to watch at the surface of the ocean.

WHAT DO YOU THINK IS THE PUBLIC APPEAL OF YOUR ANIMAL?

The Sea Otter has often been referred to as the teddy bear of the

Juvenile Sea Otter showing off webbed hind feet.

together in California to celebrate Sea Otter Awareness Week, an opportunity to share all that Sea Otters contribute to by promoting a healthier environment.

WHAT ARE YOUR HOPES FOR THE FUTURE?

Myself and others who work with Sea Otters hope that someday we will see the Southern Sea Otter return to pre-fur hunting numbers and areas of occupation along the West Coast of the United States. With many of the threats and risks facing Sea Otters over the years, including shark mortalities and diseases to name a few, we would like to see the population increase way beyond what is currently considered the number for delisting status but continue to maintain a protected status in order to sustain a healthy population. It is hopeful that several governmental and NGO agencies are working together to start the process of reintroducing otters into their formerly occupied locations in California and Oregon.

sea. It's iconic furry face as it rests peacefully in a bed of kelp while its young pup, not able to dive yet, is nestled on board nursing can often be easily spotted from shore. They often feed close to shore, or interact with pups or others in easy viewing distance and they are always entertaining. Though they may seem 'cute' to many they are still wild animals and need the proper respect with human social distancing while being watched.

WHAT HAVE BEEN YOUR BIGGEST LESSONS LEARNT?

I have learnt so many things from Sea Otters, and each time I observe them I discover something new.

Studying them as individuals has been the best lesson and has taught me how different one can be from another; their antics and personalities. Though I try not to, when I follow a wild individual for a good part of its life and get to know it a little more 'personally', it is hard not to get attached. Though it is a part of nature, when an otter you have watched for ten years is shark bitten, it is hard not to feel a sense of loss.

WHAT ARE YOUR 'STRATEGIES OF HOPE' FOR CONSERVATION?

Sea Otter research has contributed to changes in people's attitudes toward otters. Once considered a

problem in some areas because they ate 'all' the Pismo clams or urchins that were an important resource to different fishing communities who made their livelihoods harvesting these invertebrates, we are now realizing the otters' importance in the ocean. Research, education and public awareness of the important roles they play in our ecosystem — from maintaining eelgrass beds in estuaries, to carbon sequestration in the oceans by helping encourage kelp growth in their role as a keystone species — contribute to positive change in attitudes toward Southern Sea Otters along the California coast. Several organizations come

Great White Sharks

The most feared creature in the ocean, perhaps the whole world, is the **Great White Shark**. It went from infamy to mega movie-star fame as a consequence of its starring role in the movie *Jaws*, but it is far more fearsome in our imaginations than in reality. And its image as a mindless killing machine is, thankfully, changing. Not least because Jacques Cousteau and other underwater documentary makers have revealed sharks to be sleek, beautifully adapted creatures of the sea.

Great White Shark coming in for a closer look. Guadalupe Island, Mexico.

Great White Sharks are grey with a white underbelly, from where they get their name. Found throughout the world's oceans, mostly in cool waters close to the coast, their colouring serves as a type of camouflage called countershading — a feature they share with penguins — that makes them hard to see in the water. They are the largest predatory fish on our planet and, like most shark species, females grow much larger than males. Great Whites usually grow to around 4.5 metres (15 feet) long, but some have been measured at 6 metres (20 feet) — that's half the length of a bus!

Great White Sharks are some of the fastest predators in the oceans, reaching speeds up to 55 kilometres per hour (35 miles per hour). They use electromagnetic fields to feel the vibrations of potential prey in the water, and have a strong sense of smell that allows them to detect a colony of seals from over 3 kilometres (2 miles) away. In fact, if there were only one drop of blood in 100 litres (22 gallons) of water, a Great White could still smell it! They are opportunistic predators: while smaller Great Whites prey upon fish, rays and crustaceans, their larger brethren also eat seals, sea lions, dolphins, seabirds, marine turtles, rays and even other sharks.

Unlike most fish, which tend to be cold-blooded, the Great White Shark is partially warm-blooded, allowing it to adapt to different water temperatures. With a life expectancy of around 70 years, they tend to be solitary hunters and spend most of their lives alone, apart from during their mating season. Female Great Whites are pregnant for eleven months before giving

birth to a litter of around two to twelve live pups, each measuring around 1.5 metres (5 feet) in length.

Great White Sharks are at the top of the food chain and don't have natural predators, with the exception of Killer Whales, who have figured out a weak spot: sharks become motionless when flipped on their backs — a condition known as tonic immobility. Killer Whales take advantage of this condition by ramming the Great White Shark until it flips on its back and stops breathing.

Great Whites play a special role in the ocean as a top predator by keeping prey populations

Above: Great White Shark swimming amongst a school of Mackerel. Guadalupe Island, Mexico.

Opposite: Great White Shark peeping his head above the surface of the water. South Africa.

such as Elephant Seals and Sea Lions in balance. The presence of Great White Sharks, perhaps counterintuitively, provides species stability and protects the diversity of the ocean. Sadly, however, these sharks are under serious threat from human activity due to overfishing, degradation of nursing grounds, and media campaigns to kill the sharks. Great White Sharks are a Vulnerable species on the International Union for Conservation of Nature (IUCN) Red List of Threatened Species, which generally means they are likely to become endangered unless their circumstances can be improved.

As a group, sharks have been around for around 450 million years. In other words: sharks have managed to survive the four mass extinctions that have taken place on Earth since then. It would be a tragedy if these charismatic apex predators should be lost now due to our actions; a loss that would surely reverberate through the wider marine environment with negative consequences for coral reefs and almost every other species of fish. They, and we, would all be poorer should the Great White Shark not survive the world's next mass extinction — this one, which is taking place now, at the hand of humans.

Long-distance traveller — a Great White swims just beneath the calm waters of Guadalupe Island, Mexico.

Following a surface lunge, a Great White Shark begins his descent to deeper water. Guadalupe, Mexico.

CASE STUDY

California's Great White Sharks

Scott Davis, Marine Biologist/ Photographer

My research was among the first to deploy satellite tags on Great White Sharks in an effort to track the large-scale movement patterns and behaviour of individuals. Our team discovered that, contrary to previous long-held theories that they were mainly coastal and inhabited relatively shallow waters, individual Great White Sharks tagged off the coast of California travelled tremendous distances each year — in some cases, swimming all the way to the Hawaiian Islands and back. Furthermore, it's not uncommon for them to dive to great depths, to over 700 metres (2300 feet) deep. At the time, these were ground-breaking discoveries in the world of Great White Shark behaviour.

A Great White Shark breaks the surface close to the beaches and shoreline of Cape Town, South Africa.

in the hope that people will feel a desire to not only appreciate our wild creatures but also be compelled to protect, nurture and guard them for future generations.

WHAT DO YOU THINK IS THE PUBLIC APPEAL OF YOUR ANIMAL?

I think it's a mixed bag between an innate general awe and respect of a super predator through to the continued fear and misunderstanding of this mysterious and beautiful creature. More often, unfortunately, the sensationalistic narrative of this animal is that of blood and teeth and violence — and that, of course, fascinates people. Thankfully, though, there is a strong faction of conservationists, shark enthusiasts and educators out there who are attempting to illuminate for the public that this is indeed a special animal

that deserves our respect and admiration, and also our protection. This is the kind of public appeal that I'm hopeful will continue.

WHAT ARE YOUR 'STRATEGIES OF HOPE' FOR CONSERVATION?

I think one of the key elements of conservation and the choices we make come from a core appreciation of our natural world. From a very young age, I was exposed in one form or another to nature. My parents were far from outdoorsy, but they encouraged my love of nature via access to books, encouraging me to spend time outdoors and watch nature programs, and taught me the value of respect for all living things. Providing children with this core concept, I believe, goes a long way to ensuring that they make good choices later in life

WHY DO YOU DO WHAT YOU DO?

As a small boy, I loved being outside amongst all forms of nature and wildlife, but I was always fascinated by sharks and, of course, especially Great White Sharks. What initially began as a semi-fear of sharks and, more specifically, a fear of shark attacks (I loved swimming in the ocean), was soon replaced by intense

fascination. My love of nature and wildlife led me on a career path to becoming a wildlife field biologist. To this day, although my career path has now morphed from a field biologist to that of a wildlife and documentary photographer, this animal still maintains a solid source of fascination for me. As a wildlife photographer, one of my goals is to capture the uniqueness and beauty of this planet's wildlife

when it comes to conservation. It may affect how they vote for politicians or policies that are supportive of conservation, what products they purchase, or perhaps a more enlightened viewpoint that we, as a species, share this planet not only with each other but with all its wild creatures as well. If we want to survive as a planet, it's a concept we have to embrace. I realize it's a long-game strategy but if everyone gets on board, I think the chance of success is great.

WHAT ARE YOUR HOPES FOR THE FUTURE?

My hope is that we begin to think more in a collective sense. What we as individuals do to the environment in our own backyard actually has far-reaching effects and the ability to disrupt or improve the conditions of the collective whole. When we begin by making small changes individually, these individuals begin to form groups, and then the groups can become populations and this becomes movement, and on and on, until we begin to see change on a global scale. I realize it won't be easy and won't happen overnight, but through early and fact-based education, coupled with a passionate goal to protect the only home we have, I like to think we can succeed. After all, there really isn't a back-up plan if we irreparably mess up this planet.

Full display of the speed and power of a Great White Shark during a breaching attack. South Africa.

Escaping from the flies and insects on the ground and perhaps to gain a better view of their surroundings, two female lions take to the high branches of a tree for a mid-afternoon siesta. Lake Nakuru, Kenya.

CHAPTER 7

Big Cats

Being a crowd favourite is no guarantee of immortality. Despite their global appeal, Big Cats continue to decline in numbers. One gross (in every way) measure of the consequence of how we show our love for them inappropriately: there are between 5000 and 7000 tigers kept in captivity in the United States — often as private pets — compared to fewer than 3900 tigers remaining in the wild.

The lion has forever been a symbol of strength, power and ferocity. Often known as the 'king of the jungle', ironically, most lions live in the savannah or grasslands — at least the ones not living in India. These majestic cats are threatened by habitat loss and are listed as Vulnerable on the IUCN Red List of Threatened Species. **African Lions** are the second largest of the Big Cats, with the tiger being the largest. Males can reach a shoulder height of around

Left: Cheetah family on patrol. Botswana.

Opposite: Portrait of a male lion. Zambia.

1.2 metres (4 feet) and weigh anything from 150 to 227 kilograms (330 to 500 pounds). Females are somewhat smaller, standing just over 0.90 metres (3 feet) at the shoulder and typically weighing a comparatively svelte 125 kilograms (275 pounds). A good gauge of a male lion's age is the darkness of his mane. The darker the mane, the older the lion. The mane is not the only thing to change: lion cubs are born with blue eyes that change to amber or brown when they are two to three months old.

Lions hunt a wide variety of game including buffalo, wildebeest, zebra and gemsboks, and even young elephants and hippos. Lions are the most sociable member of the cat family and can be found living in prides of up to 25 individuals. Male lions defend the pride's territory while the females do most of the hunting. Female lions typically stay in the pride in which they were born, whereas young males eventually leave the pride and attempt to join another pride for breeding. Males taking over a pride often kill small cubs so that the mothers will be free to mate with them and thereby ensure their own genes prevail. Lions have one of the most complex communication behaviours of any of the cats. They can make a variety of calls, which include roars, grunts, moans, growls, snarls,

Left: A young lion cub playing on a tree. Botswana.

Opposite: A mother cheetah with her young cubs looks for danger on the grassy savannahs of the Masai Mara, Kenya.

meows, purrs, hums, puffs and woofs. If the lion is the king of anything, it is the king of the roar: it is the loudest of any Big Cat and can be heard over 8 kilometres (5 miles) away. They roar to advertise territorial ownership, intimidate rivals, locate other members of the pride, and assist in social cohesion.

Cheetahs — the fastest land mammals on the planet — are as endearing as they are incredible. They can reach speeds of 110 kilometres per hour (70 miles per hour) in under

three seconds, performance that is worthy of a top sports car. Their bodies have evolved for speed, with long legs, an elongated spine, claws adapted for gripping the ground, and a long tail for balance. Like tigers and lions, being a beloved and charismatic species is no recipe for success: since the turn of the twentieth century, the population of cheetahs has declined by 90 per cent and almost all the blame can be laid at our feet. Reasons include habitat loss and degradation, human–wildlife conflict, and an

illegal trade in cheetahs. Even having the highest reproduction rates out of the entire Big Cat family is no protection, as nearly 90 per cent of cheetah cubs die within their first three months. The cheetah, like the lion, is now classified as Vulnerable.

Snow Leopards are the most mysterious and elusive of the Big Cats. They live in harsh, snowy and rugged alpine regions in central and southern Asia at elevations between around 3000 and 5000 metres (10,000 and 17,000 feet)

across a total of twelve different countries. The ideal Snow Leopard habitat is bleak, dangerous, cold and desolate — not most people's idea of a nice place to live. Only some 4000 Snow Leopards remain in the wild. Poaching, habitat loss and retaliatory killings due to loss of livestock are threatening their survival too.

Snow Leopards are often called the 'ghosts of the mountain' because they are so rarely seen and spend most of their lives in solitude. The fur on their stomachs is nearly 13 centimetres (5 inches) thick to help them survive in the cold mountain environment. Their thick, massive tails, which help them maintain balance as they negotiate precarious slopes, are almost as long as their entire body. Perhaps most surprising of all, Snow Leopards' tails are so thick because they contain fat that is used to get the animal through lean times.

Snow Leopards can jump up to 15 metres (50 feet) and, unbelievably, up to 6 metres (20 feet) vertically — as high as a two-storey house! Sadly, even that is not enough to escape the reach of the illegal wildlife traders.

Above: The distinctive patterns of a Snow Leopard's fur.

Opposite: Large male lion with cub. Botswana.

CASE STUDY

Developing genetic tools to help us protect the Big Cats

Natalie Schmitt, Conservation Geneticist

For the last three years I've been working to develop a genetic technology that will revolutionize global conservation of Snow Leopards and other animals: technology that fits into the palm of your hand and, through a simple colour change that takes place within 30 minutes, can tell us whether we have genetic material from a species of interest, be it faecal matter, skin, hair or potentially bone. Finding simple, inexpensive ways to identify the remains of wildlife is crucial to identifying illegally trafficked wildlife products and monitoring elusive species in the wild. With the loss of biodiversity increasing at such an alarming rate, I'm passionate about developing simple technological solutions for everyday conservation problems, which can allow greater global participation in monitoring and understanding our precious wildlife.

WHY DO YOU DO WHAT YOU DO?

For as long as I can remember I've had such an intense love for animals. They are the most vulnerable amongst us and they need our protection, not just for themselves, but for our survival also. My journey and purpose have been to discover ways that I can best help them, whether that be through scientific research, working with and empowering communities to conserve wildlife, or inspiring the public to see our interconnectedness so we value wildlife as we would any important person in our lives.

WHAT DO YOU THINK IS THE PUBLIC APPEAL OF YOUR ANIMAL?

Snow Leopards are fascinating. They epitomize strength, ethereal beauty, nobility, prowess, mystique and wonder. They have this feminine energy about them and, in many ways, I aspire to be like them as a woman myself.

Natalie Schmitt (far right) with colleagues working in the field in Lower Mustang, Nepal.

A Snow Leopard: ever-attentive, even in the rain.

WHAT HAVE BEEN YOUR BIGGEST LESSONS LEARNT?

To trust in my heart and be open to directions and paths I might never have considered. This has been crucial in conquering the voices of doubt and trepidation I've felt as an independent scientist in my battle to fund and develop new technology that was almost completely outside my field of expertise.

WHAT ARE YOUR 'STRATEGIES OF HOPE' FOR CONSERVATION?

I've realized that one of the most powerful tools we have as conservation scientists is that of human connection: to engage effectively with the public and inspire positive change in the world. We scientists should not be afraid to show our humanity; to express our joys, fears, heartbreak and love for the work we do. This authenticity is what people relate to first and foremost, which in turn, can inspire them to care about the planet as we do.

WHAT ARE YOUR HOPES FOR THE FUTURE?

My eternal hope is that humanity comes to realize we are not separate from nature, but rather an intrinsic part of it. Nature is us, physically and spiritually. If we can learn new ways to reconnect with each other and nature, I truly believe we are capable of such immense positive changes for the planet.

CHAPTER 8

Elephants

Elephants are the largest land animals on Earth, and they are one of the most unique-looking animals too. Watching elephants move in a large herd across an arid terrain is almost hypnotic, as if they are moving to a rhythm where only they can hear the music. With their characteristic long trunks, large floppy ears and thick legs, their physique is like that of no other animal.

There are two species of elephant in the world: the **Asian Elephant** and the **African Elephant**. African Elephants come in two types: the forest and savannah subspecies. Male African Elephants can be up to 3.9 metres (13 feet) tall and weigh up to 8 tonnes. Asian Elephants are slightly smaller, at under 2.7 metres (9 feet) tall and weighing between 3 and 6 tonnes. An elephant lives on average about 70 years — similar to us humans.

Sadly, elephants are in trouble. Many are killed by humans for their ivory tusks, or because they've come into conflict with communities or,

Drinking up to 190 litres (50 gallons) of water a day, elephants return to a river source for their daily drink. Kenya.

Left: Young elephants at play in the river. Samburu National Park, Kenya.

Right: A protective matriarch elephant stands guard over her family herd. Botswana.

tragically, simply for sport. Despite international sanctions against trading in ivory, unfortunately the demand for ivory — especially from Asia — has fuelled what amounts to war by poachers against the elephants. In Africa alone, poachers killed 100,000 elephants over a three-year period just for their tusks. That is a huge portion of the population of African Elephants, now estimated to be 415,000, and they are now classified as Vulnerable. The even less populous Asian Elephants, of which there are fewer than 50,000, are categorized as Endangered.

The elephant's gestation period is 22 months — longer than any other land animal — and a newborn elephant baby can weigh over 110 kilograms (243 pounds)! Seemingly defying gravity, the baby is able to stand up shortly after birth.

Elephants appear to relish water and can swim using their trunks as a snorkel. The trunk is also used to drink, smell, pick up food, touch and communicate. Elephants can pick up trees with their trunks, but they can also use their trunks for remarkably delicate manoeuvres, such as picking up a coin.

Being such large animals and living in the open, they need strategies for dealing with the

sun. Their large ears are used to radiate excess heat away from their bodies. They have even created their very own form of sunscreen: when bathing, they suck water to spray on their bodies, which they then cover with dirt and mud.

Elephants are highly social animals and live in strong family units. The leader of a herd is usually the oldest female, the matriarch. She is both leader and protector, and will even chase away lions. Females spend their entire lives in a group of related females that can include mothers, grandmothers, aunts, sisters and daughters. Adult males, by comparison, often adopt a bachelor lifestyle.

Elephant behaviour exudes a great deal of the intelligence that underlies it: elephants display grief, altruism, compassion, self-awareness, playfulness and, arguably, even art. They have excellent memories and they can show fierce loyalty. When a family member dies, they give every indication of appearing to mourn its death. Given that we are supposedly blessed with similar levels of intelligence and sensitivity, we should mourn the death of every elephant too!

A herd of elephants traverses the dry plains of Amboseli National Park, Kenya.

CASE STUDY

Reteti Elephant Sanctuary and Community Empowerment

Christina Geijer, Conservation Biologist; Katie Rowe, Co-founder Reteti Elephant Sanctuary; and Dorothy Lowekutuk, Reteti Wildlife Keeper

Below: Christina Geijer in the field.
Bottom: Katie Rowe (left) and Dorothy Lowekutuk (right) working at Reteti Elephant Sanctuary.

The Reteti Elephant Sanctuary is in northern Kenya and is the first community-owned elephant orphanage in Africa. It is a representation of communities standing up and uniting for wildlife; a recognition of the value that elephants can cultivate. Opportunities are being created, livelihoods are improving, and wildlife is returning — proving that nature can provide a sustainable economy for the populations that occupy its magnificent ecosystem. The orphaned elephants that are cared for by the Samburu keepers like Dorothy are symbols of a new wave of thinking about wildlife and the environment, which goes far beyond traditional conservation methods. On a fast-developing continent where space is at a premium, the Samburu community that occupies the Namunyak Wildlife Conservancy is reversing the past trends of environmental degradation and loss of wildlife by securing their wilderness landscapes, returning to a learned, age-old history of wildlife tolerance and co-existence. Katie Rowe is one of the co-founders of Reteti, as well as being instrumental in the training of the keepers and building the systems to allow for the day-to-day running of the project. Dr Christina Geijer has been part of the project from when it was just a conversation around a coffee table. She has written the Management Plans and Standard Operating Procedures for the sanctuary for the Kenya Wildlife Service and other key partners.

WHY DO YOU DO WHAT YOU DO?

Christina: I'm my happiest and most peaceful self when in nature with animals, and it breaks my heart to see the natural world being destroyed. While at university in the United Kingdom, I volunteered for a variety of conservation projects in Kenya, which led to a Master's degree and PhD in conservation science. Becoming involved with Reteti has been a wonderful opportunity to work with elephants, but also to learn about the community model of conservation in northern Kenya.

Katie: Living in the wilderness of north Kenya I can see first-hand the positive impact elephants have on the environment around us. When elephants falter, we also falter, and we need to relearn how to share the landscape peacefully. But Reteti isn't just about saving elephants, it's also about breaking down stereotypes and redefining

Right: Under the protection of his mother, a young elephant quenches his thirst. Samburu National Park, Kenya.

wildlife management: it is changing the way communities view the wildlife around them. When people realize that they can benefit from healthy elephant populations, they are proud to take care of wildlife. We are really pioneering a new model of community-owned conservation.

Dorothy: I love the work. I love being busy and I am inspired to learn every day. Katie has taught me this work and I love working with a team of strong women; we encourage and inspire each other.

WHAT DO YOU THINK IS THE PUBLIC APPEAL OF YOUR ANIMAL?

Christina: What makes elephants exceptional is their intelligence, emotional sensitivity and strong family bonding. In terms of public appeal, I would love to enhance people's understanding of all the things that unite us with this spectacular species. Then true compassion can arise for the need to protect them.

Katie: Elephants are extraordinarily caring and of course more intelligent than we can understand. They are magnificent to observe in the wild and hold strong family values. I think we can learn a lot from them! When watching orphans interact it's hard not to fall in love with the way they play and throw mud around, completely carefree.

Dorothy: They are just like human beings with personalities and should be treated as we expect to be treated. When they are having fun, their personalities shine through: they love to play and let themselves be free.

WHAT HAVE BEEN YOUR BIGGEST LESSONS LEARNT?

Christina: Conservation starts and ends with human behaviour. We don't manage animals as much as we manage human attitudes, human threats and human ability (or lack thereof) for conservation leadership. From local people to the general public, the business sector and government, human behaviour needs to change to appreciate the innate value of conserving nature.

Katie: We need collaboration on all levels, from the grass roots to the top levels; we need to work together and respect fellow humans and understand their challenges. We need the courage to persist, knowing that however hard the day ahead looks, the future is full of hope .

Dorothy: The best part of the elephants is the love they have towards humans: they feel happy when we are happy and sad when we are sad. We are connected.

WHAT ARE YOUR 'STRATEGIES OF HOPE' FOR CONSERVATION?

Christina: I believe a strategy of hope for conservation lies with empowering local women as leaders. In the world of conservation, women are largely an untapped resource with immense potential. Reteti has really embodied this, by empowering and training local women as caretakers of rescued elephant calves.

Katie: I believe in an all-inclusive approach to conservation, breaking down stereotypes, and increasing collaboration. Conservation can't be territorial — we don't have the time.

Dorothy: My strategy of hope is to change the ecosystem of the Samburu area and improve the living standards of wild animals, and that the next generations will follow this idea and improve upon it generation after generation.

WHAT ARE YOUR HOPES FOR THE FUTURE?

Christina: With regards to conservation, I am seeing a gradual shift of values in society. More people from different walks of life are becoming involved. This is a good

trend, and in many countries it has started to filter into governmental policy change, albeit at too slow a rate and with some notable setbacks. My biggest hope lies with strong environmental laws coupled with local leadership, ensuring local people have the vision, education, management capacity and financial flows to conserve the wildlife with which they live side by side.

Katie: I hope Reteti will help protect this wilderness for generations to come by providing jobs and educating communities on the importance of their grasslands, forests and watersheds. We all do better when the landscape is healthy, and when people see and fully understand that people thrive when nature thrives. I hope that can become a blueprint for other projects all over the world to follow the same values and ideas.

Dorothy: I hope to see our children seeing benefits from Reteti and supporting nature and wildlife to support their children too.

An elephant herd gathering around a local watering hole for an afternoon drink. Botswana.

CHAPTER 9

Giraffes

Imagine an African safari without seeing a giraffe: it just wouldn't be Africa without these gentle giants striding around the savannah. The giraffe is the tallest mammal now walking the Earth, standing up to 5.7 metres (18 feet 8 inches) high. That's more than 1 metre (3 feet) higher than a double-decker bus. Just their legs, at over 1.8 metres (6 feet), are taller than most humans — heck, even a newborn baby giraffe is too. Despite being incredibly tall and having incredibly long necks, giraffes still only have seven vertebrae in their necks, the exact same number of bones as us.

A giraffe's spots are much like human fingerprints: no two giraffes have the same pattern. It is thought that the pattern on a giraffe doesn't just serve to camouflage the animal, but also helps with temperature regulation too. Despite being relatively long, a giraffe's neck is actually too short to reach the ground given the size of its legs. As a consequence, the giraffe has to awkwardly spread its front legs or kneel to reach the ground for a drink of water. Luckily, they get most of their water from the plants they eat and only need to drink water every few

Grouped together, these four giraffes can keep an eye out for danger in every direction. Serengeti National Park, Tanzania.

days. Giraffes have some of the biggest feet in the animal kingdom, each having a diameter of 30 centimetres (1 foot), the size of a dinner plate. These massive hooves are used to distribute their weight, preventing them from sinking into sand or marshy areas.

Giraffes actually share something in common with some of the world's smallest creatures, bees: they are exceptional pollinators. Their great height and super long tongues for feeding in treetops mean that they transfer pollen onto

their mouths, and then from one flower of a tree to another. A giraffe's tongue is a whopping 50 centimetres (20 inches) long and is deep purple in colour due to dark melanin pigment.

Giraffes have the same amount of teeth as humans, however, all of their front teeth are on the bottom of their mouth! There are mostly molars positioned right at the back. Giraffes use their bottom teeth and tongue to grab a branch and then comb the leaves off. They spend most of their lives standing up and rarely lie down to

sleep, as this would make them vulnerable to predators. Instead, they take micro-naps while lying down, curling their necks around to rest on their hindquarters for a quick five minutes of shut-eye, and rarely sleep more than 30 minutes at a time.

A female giraffe's gestation period lasts for fifteen months and, because she gives birth standing up, her newborn will start its life with a mini sky dive, falling almost 2 metres (6 feet) to the ground. Mothers will bravely attempt to

A lone giraffe crosses the parched plains of Amboseli National Park, Kenya.

Two Reticulated Giraffes. Northern Kenya.

protect their calves from attacks by lions, hyenas and leopards by standing over them. Even so, many calves are killed in their first few months.

Giraffes are sadly declining in the wild, due mainly to habitat loss caused by increasing agriculture and poaching for their prized tail hair, pelts and meat. As a consequence, they are now extinct in eight African countries where they previously roamed. Fortunately, there are many conservation groups leading the charge to support the giraffes and ensure their survival.

Save the Giraffes

Fred Bercovitch, Wildlife Biologist

I am fascinated by both evolution and conservation. The fundamental problem today is that of continued human population growth in combination with a finite level of resources, so that many animals are at risk of disappearing from the planet. Can they adjust to changes in the landscape when people have devastated their homelands? Where can they go? Conservation science can provide political leaders, local people, stakeholders and business operations with guidelines as to how we might save species if we know more about those species.

WHY DO YOU DO WHAT YOU DO?

Since I was in kindergarten, I've wanted to be Tarzan. I have spent my life travelling to different locations to study animals, and at the same time sharing knowledge about animals. At the heart of all of this is my amazement at the diversity of life on Earth and my insatiable desire to share my wonder and excitement about nature with other people.

WHAT DO YOU THINK IS THE PUBLIC APPEAL OF YOUR ANIMAL?

In 1981, Sir Peter Medawar, a recipient of the Nobel Prize in Physiology or Medicine, wrote: 'Few animals are more endearing than baby giraffes'. People are mesmerized by giraffes, especially their eyes and neck, but the gangly appearance of a newborn infant, and its exuberance for prancing about, are certainly an added

Fred Bercovitch working in the field.

delight to most people. Many of the traits that make the babies cute remain into adulthood, most notably the long eyelashes and the huge, dark brown eyes. They never have sad eyes; they are always wide open, eyes that seem to be watching us as we watch them.

WHAT HAVE BEEN YOUR BIGGEST LESSONS LEARNT, AND WHAT ARE YOUR 'STRATEGIES OF HOPE' FOR CONSERVATION?

My strategy for the future is like a three-legged stool in that it involves three items forming a base: one leg is conservation education of both children and adults in the host country. We have to provide people with a reason to save species. The second leg is conservation education at nearly the opposite end: people in developed and advanced countries who can afford to go to zoos and wildlife parks. Captive animals are ambassadors for their species and can raise money for conservation in the wild. Both of these legs are built upon a foundation that learning about the life and plight of giraffes, and exposure to these magnificent beasts, can help save them for future generations. And therein lies the essence of the third leg: field research that documents the factors and forces that regulate the feeding and reproductive activity of giraffes in the wild. This offers a solid foundation for conservation education of the public, and for designing and developing conservation management plans.

WHAT ARE YOUR HOPES FOR THE FUTURE?

My ultimate hope is that non-profit conservation organizations saving animals go out of business. If animals are not threatened with extinction, then organizations devoted to saving them from extinction will be unnecessary. My way to try to achieve that goal is mostly through conservation education, especially aimed at younger people. When the leaders of tomorrow absorb and adapt a lifestyle conducive to conservation of biodiversity, we will have a promising future that can protect our precious planet.

Giraffe with characteristic long eyelashes and large eyes.

Opposite: A giraffe grazes the tree tops, using its long tongue to grab leaves.

Kangaroos

Kangaroos are among the world's most iconic species. Beautiful and adorably bizarre at the same time, they are an evolutionary marvel: the only large animal that hops! **Kangaroos** can easily be identified by their muscular tail, large feet, strong back legs and long, pointed ears. Like all marsupials, female kangaroos have a pouch on their belly to carry and nurse baby kangaroos, called joeys.

Kangaroos are indigenous to Australia and are emblematic of Australia's unique biodiversity. Kangaroos and their affiliates (wallabies, pademelons and tree kangaroos) are so diverse that they have been dubbed Australia's most successful evolutionary product, with over 50 different species spread across the country. If nearby New Guinea is included, the number of kangaroo species jumps to more than 70.

The largest kangaroo is the **Red Kangaroo**, standing over 1.8 metres (6 feet) tall. Large males can weigh up to 90 kilograms (200 pounds), while females typically weigh in at less than

Red Kangaroo with baby joey in pouch. Female Red Kangaroos are sometimes known as blue flyers.

Chilling out, Red Kangaroo style.

Right: A Red Kangaroo in the grasslands of the Australian outback.

45 kilograms (100 pounds). Kangaroos are social and live in groups called a mob, a herd or a troop. Members of a mob will groom and protect each other from danger. If threatened, kangaroos pound the ground with their strong feet to warn the others in the group. Their charismatic charm is not to be messed with, however: when they fight, they punch and kick with powerful blows, and will sometimes even bite.

Newborn joeys are tiny, measuring just 2.5 centimetres (1 inch) long, or about the size of a grape. After birth, joeys travel unassisted through their mother's thick fur to the comfort and safety of the pouch. A newborn cannot suckle or swallow, so the kangaroo mother contracts muscles around her pouch to pump milk down its throat. At around seven months, the youngster emerges from the pouch for short trips, and by ten months it is mature enough to leave the pouch for good.

Thanks to their large feet and powerful hind legs, the largest kangaroos can travel at more than 70 kilometres per hour (43 miles per hour) and leap more than 9 metres (30 feet) in a single bound. They hop because they have to: most species, with the exception of the tree kangaroos, cannot move their legs independently very well. The length of their hind feet and the weight of their tail make walking difficult, although some species can shuffle on all fours using their tail as a sort of fifth leg, and a line of ancient giant sthenurine kangaroos — which died out 30,000 years ago — walked on their long hind legs, being way too heavy to hop.

For most of the world's charismatic species, their attractive nature has been

Left: Family portrait —
mother and joey Eastern Grey
Kangaroo.

Opposite: Home sweet home
— a Grey Kangaroo joey
inside its mother's pouch.

something of a curse, endangering them from all the attention we give them in one form or another. And while that also holds for some of the smaller and lesser-known kangaroo species, most of the larger species (the Red, **Eastern Grey** and **Western Grey Kangaroos** and the **Common Wallaroo** have the opposite problem, with their numbers increasing dramatically. One reason for this is that female kangaroos are pretty much perpetually reproducing: females can pause the development of a new embryo until the current joey is able to leave the pouch. Once it does, she resumes her pregnancy and the cycle repeats itself. Add to that continuous production line an absence of large predators, such as dingoes (which have become locally extinct in many areas), and this has resulted

in what some consider to be plague-like numbers of kangaroos. In some areas, there are up to 800 kangaroos per square mile. The unchecked population growth of the kangaroos is destroying native ecosystems, damaging crops, competing with livestock for food, and resulting in a high number of collisions with cars each year.

This, however, is where the kangaroo's charismatic status does it no favours. The management of overabundant native mammals is a contentious issue in Australia and the iconic status of these kangaroos, nationally and internationally, greatly influences the public perception of what are acceptable wildlife management practices. Since 1984, the Australian government has sanctioned the harvesting of the above four species of

kangaroos across large areas of Australia, but this has met with an outcry from people appalled at the culling of these cute and iconic creatures. Campaigners outside Australia have successfully managed to ban the importation of kangaroo meat and fur products. This threatens to make harvesting uneconomic and puts in jeopardy a large swathe of other native animals and plants that are being annihilated by the population explosion of kangaroos.

Kangaroos are the national symbol of Australia, but the country has a complicated relationship with its mascot. As with most things biological, the future of the roos and the unique biodiversity of Australia depend upon reaching some sort of balance, which means bringing the unchecked population growth of some kangaroo species into line.

CASE STUDY

The reproduction of Eastern Grey Kangaroos

Marco Festa-Bianchet, Evolutionary Ecologist

Our long-term study of Eastern Grey Kangaroos is based upon monitoring of marked individuals, ideally from birth to death. We began in 2008 and have monitored over 1200 individuals. The research aims to study their population ecology, individual reproductive success, and evolutionary ecology. We are particularly interested in the effects of early development on lifetime reproductive success. This is a high-density population so our research is relevant for conservation of kangaroos in areas with no predators.

WHY DO YOU DO WHAT YOU DO?

I have always been interested in animals and so I studied zoology at university. I was not really interested in an academic career at first, but after working for the government for a couple of years, I realized that what I really wanted to do was research; to find out new stuff. I like to monitor individual animals and discover what happens over their entire lifetime. Kangaroos make a fascinating subject because of the way the female is in control of lactation and can decide whether to continue with it depending upon resource availability.

WHAT DO YOU THINK IS THE PUBLIC APPEAL OF YOUR ANIMAL?

It has to be the young with the head sticking out of its mother's pouch. I also think it's just how 'different' kangaroos are from anything else that people outside Australia are familiar with: a large mammal that hops on two feet and has a rhythmic bounding gait with a huge tail for balancing. And the somewhat human-like arms and hands. Finally, it is so much a symbol of Australia, that most people associate its familiar shape with the country as a whole.

WHAT ARE YOUR BIGGEST LESSONS LEARNT?

Probably the fact that one cannot learn much about kangaroos with just one or two years of monitoring a single female, because her reproduction that year is affected by what she did the year before and will affect what she may do the following year. Among the surprises we found was the fact that the large, dominant males do not monopolize paternities: a lot of young are sired by the many males in the 40 to 50 kilogram (90 to 110 pound) range, although larger males (which can be up to 75 kilograms/165 pounds) definitely do better. The enormous year-to-year variability in reproductive success, and particularly the variation in juvenile survival, was even greater than I expected. Finally, I really did not expect to discover that about 3 per cent of young are adopted by another female at about seven to nine months of age and continue to be nursed by their adoptive mother for another nine to ten months.

WHAT ARE YOUR 'STRATEGIES OF HOPE' FOR CONSERVATION?

Conservation of kangaroos is complicated because the larger species are generally very abundant and, in some cases, considered pests, but many of the smaller species are endangered by habitat loss and introduced predators. For the larger species, overabundance is often the main problem, with negative effects on many other grassland species, from plants to ground-nesting birds, to small reptiles that need vegetation for cover. In these areas, I am in favour of humane commercial harvesting, which can make kangaroos valuable for farmers and should discourage their persecution. I am dismayed by campaigns against the commercial use of kangaroo products, which I see as a win–win for farmers and conservation. I think this is a case where the iconic status of kangaroos as a symbol of Australia actually damages their conservation because it makes urbanites unwilling to support sustainable harvesting needed to keep the populations in check. For the smaller species, habitat protection and predator control are necessary. Like most life on Earth, all kangaroos are threatened by climate change and the increases in fires and drought that it brings about. My hope is for societal and political changes that will lead to effective strategies to reverse the production of greenhouse gases.

WHAT ARE YOUR HOPES FOR THE FUTURE?

My main hope is for more restored ecosystems where populations of large kangaroos are limited by dingo predation and smaller species are not exposed to predation from introduced cats and foxes. For areas where dingoes have been extirpated, I hope for conservation of large kangaroos through integration in economic production systems, giving value to these species and ensuring their persistence while limiting their adverse impacts on both ecosystems and farming. Kangaroo meat has great potential as a source of protein that does not have the same implications of habitat destruction as beef or lamb. Because they are not ruminants, kangaroos also do not produce much methane, a powerful greenhouse gas emitted by cows and sheep.

A tight squeeze: large Eastern Grey Kangaroo joey still enjoying a free ride.

CHAPTER 11

Koalas

Chapter co-written with Lloyd Spencer Davis

If charisma were an element like carbon or oxygen that could be measured accurately, then **Koalas** would be composed of 100 per cent charisma. No other animal combines cuteness, cuddliness, uniqueness and apparent placidity to the same extent. The Koala is a well-known and popular animal, native to Australia but recognized around the world. Despite often being called 'koala bears', like kangaroos, Koalas are marsupials and have pouches. The closest relative of the Koala is the wombat.

The Koala: the ultimate combination of cute-appeal and charisma.

Koalas are tree-dwelling with large, furry ears, a prominent black nose, long sharp claws adapted for climbing, and no tail. They live in eucalyptus forests, where they eat mainly eucalyptus leaves, munching through almost 1 kilogram (2 pounds) or more of the leaves each day. Eucalyptus is poisonous to most animals, but Koalas use the microorganisms in their specialized fibre-digesting organ, the caecum, to detoxify the chemicals in the leaves. The reputation of the Koala as the model for a soft and cuddly children's toy is partially earned by its docile appearance. Living off a diet of eucalyptus leaves is hard work, as the leaves are fibrous and have very low nutritional value, so Koalas don't have much energy to spare. As a consequence, when not feasting on leaves they spend most of their time dozing in the branches. They can sleep for up to eighteen hours a day!

When an infant Koala — called a joey — is born, it looks like a hairless pink jellybean and weighs less than 1 gram (or 1/25th of an ounce). It immediately climbs up to its mother's pouch; blind and earless, the joey uses its strong sense of touch and smell, as well as a genetically determined instinct for direction, to find its way through its mother's fur to her pouch. Once inside, the joey latches on to one of the two teats, which swells to fill its mouth, ensuring the joey always has milk on tap. The joey stays in the pouch suckling for about six months. When it is six to seven months old, its mum supplements the milk with 'pap', a soft form of special poo she produces, which passes onto the youngster the necessary microorganisms needed to digest

Above: The claws of the Koala are like crampons for tree climbing.

Left: Koalas and eucalyptus trees: the aerial equivalents of pigs and mud.

the eucalyptus leaves that will constitute its diet as an adult Koala. Once out of the pouch, the youngster rides around on its mother's back for a further six months or so, lying on her stomach for the occasional milk drink (as it is now too big to get in the pouch, remarkably its mother's teat elongates so that it sticks out of the pouch for easy access) and beginning to feed on fresh eucalyptus leaves.

Not everything about eating its mother's poo is good for the young Koala. Koalas are particularly vulnerable to a sexually transmitted disease, chlamydia, which can cause blindness, infertility and death. It is transmitted between Koalas when they mate, but can also be passed

onto the young Koala in its mother's pap. In some populations, infection rates can be as high as 100 per cent. Fortunately, recent research has shown that a vaccine and an antibiotic, doxycycline, may be effective at treating chlamydia infections. Yet while this STD remains a serious issue for Koalas, they face more significant problems.

Prior to the European settlement of Australia, Koalas were undoubtedly more widespread and abundant than they are now. Habitat loss, through the clearing of eucalyptus forests, has been largely responsible for the reduction in their current distribution and numbers. In some parts of Australia, such as New South Wales and Queensland, numbers of Koalas have reduced substantially since 1990, leading to Koalas being listed as Vulnerable by the International Union for the Conservation of Nature. It is hard to even estimate current Koala numbers in the wild, let alone census them, but there are likely to be between 300,000 to 600,000 Koalas left in Australia.

Ironically, in some parts of Australia, such as Victoria and South Australia, Koala populations are burgeoning and in danger of outstripping their food supply. At Cape Otway, on Victoria's southern coast, a sustainable density of Koalas is estimated to be less than one Koala for every hectare (2½ acres) of eucalyptus forest, but numbers got as high as twenty Koalas per hectare and many died of starvation. This prompted the government to authorize the euthanizing of nearly 700 Koalas that were in imminent danger of starving to death. However, if culling kangaroos wasn't controversial enough, nobody kills the King of Charisma without media outcry, even if the intention is to prevent pain and suffering — word got out and an international outcry has resulted in much scrutiny of Koala management programs.

Researchers have been scrambling to find other ways to control the numbers of Koalas. The most promising avenue so far? Contraceptive implants.

Koala contraception for wildlife management

Emily Hynes, Wildlife Ecologist

Koala conservation poses a conundrum. There are many populations, particularly in the north of the Koalas' range, where numbers are declining. In contrast, there are populations in southern Australia where Koalas are so numerous that they can overeat their preferred eucalyptus food trees. Without management intervention, this can lead to death of the tress and starvation for the Koalas. In these circumstances, the biggest threat to Koala habitat and survival is the Koalas themselves.

I research and implement non-lethal methods of controlling high-density Koala populations, such as using contraceptive implants, which can result in lifelong contraception in female Koalas with no adverse impacts on their behaviour or health, in order to slow population growth. These implants are now used to manage many Koala populations in southern Australia. Translocation is another management technique used to reduce Koala densities in locations where they are overeating their food trees. I have investigated the survival, health and movements of Koalas after they have been released into new areas, so as to inform future decisions about where Koalas can be released successfully.

WHY DO YOU DO WHAT YOU DO?

I have always loved animals and felt happier in the bush than in the city, so working in wildlife ecology was a natural career path for me. I ended up falling into Koala research after I was offered a PhD at the University of Melbourne. My career in Koala research has flowed on from there. I've always loved heights so the opportunity to climb trees is an appealing part of my work. Being in the canopy of a tree provides a unique perspective on the forest.

WHAT DO YOU THINK IS THE PUBLIC APPEAL OF YOUR ANIMAL?

Koalas have the classic characteristics that stimulate protective instincts in humans. They have forward-facing eyes and similar dimensions to a human baby. When a Koala is in its normal sitting position, on its rump with its legs tucked up, its head-to-body ratio is similar to a twelve- or eighteen-month-old human baby. This stimulates an innate response in humans to nurture and protect them. There is also

Scientists climbing eucalyptus trees to study Koalas.

an innocence in the way that Koalas sit still and stare at you from a tree. The cuteness factor grows exponentially when a mother has a baby on its back.

WHAT HAVE BEEN YOUR BIGGEST LESSONS LEARNT?

I come from a scientific background so I used to think that people would listen to, and be motivated to act on, evidence-based reasoning. However, I have come to understand that even the best scientific evidence often won't overcome political and societal influences and preconceived perceptions of a situation. Rather than just bombarding people with facts and data, conservation scientists need to engage with communities and try to understand things from their perspective. In addition, I've learnt that personal stories and a focus on individual animals engages the public more effectively than numbers and science.

WHAT ARE YOUR 'STRATEGIES OF HOPE' FOR CONSERVATION?

Cute, charismatic species like Koalas are part of interconnected ecosystems made up of countless organisms. To conserve Koalas, we need to look after the whole ecosystem. Although Koalas are only one part of the system, I believe that the passion they invoke in people can be harnessed to motivate behavioural changes that will benefit many species. For example, climate change is one of the biggest threats to the survival of Koalas. Educating people about the impacts of climate change on Koalas can motivate them to reduce their carbon emissions, leading to benefits for countless species, including humans.

WHAT ARE YOUR HOPES FOR THE FUTURE?

I hope that through my work, and the work of other scientists and conservationists, more people will develop an awareness of the interconnectedness of nature and our place in it. I hope that this inspires people to fight to protect nature and appreciate that we need to share the planet with other species if we are to have a hope of surviving into the future.

Whale Sharks

It's not a whale, it's a fish! Nevertheless, **Whale Sharks** act more like whales than sharks in some ways. They swim about with their mouths wide open, filter feeding, not eating the big fish, seals or the odd human limb that we associate with feeding by other sharks.

The Whale Shark is, in fact, the largest fish in the entire ocean, growing up to 15 metres (50 feet) long and tipping the scales at over 20 tonnes. But far from being a dangerous man-eater, its favourite meal consists of some of the tiniest creatures in the ocean: plankton. Even though Whale Sharks have 300 rows of minuscule teeth, they do not use them for feeding. Instead, they open their colossal mouths — which are about 1.5 metres (5 feet) wide — and suck in water,

The speckled topcoat of the Whale Shark.

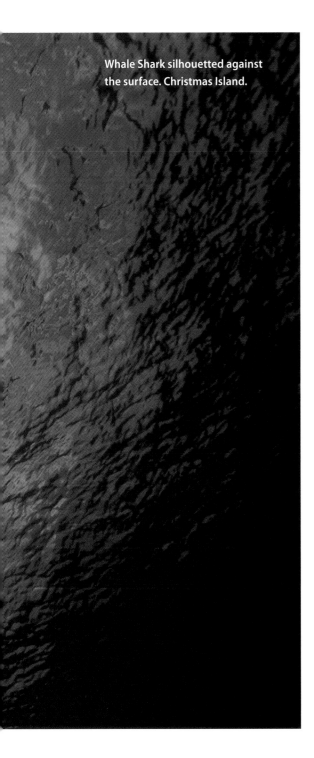

Whale Shark silhouetted against the surface. Christmas Island.

sieving out the plankton and any small fish swimming close to the sea's surface.

It must be a healthy diet because Whale Sharks can live up to 100 years or longer. They reach sexual maturity when they're about 30 years old. The eggs of the Whale Shark remain in the body of the females, which give birth to live young that are only 40 to 60 centimetres (16 to 24 inches) long.

Whale Sharks tend to like warmer areas and are found in tropical waters all over the world.

Each Whale Shark has its own unique pattern of spots, which can be used to identify it, much like human fingerprints or the patterning on giraffes. Their populations have reduced dramatically over the last 75 years, with numbers in the Indian and Pacific Oceans dropping by 63 per cent and those in the Atlantic faring only a little better, with a reduction in their numbers of over 30 per cent. Worse still: the populations are continuing to decrease and because of this Whale Sharks are classified as Endangered.

They are called Whale Sharks for a reason — this human diver is dwarfed by the big fish.

The biggest danger to Whale Sharks is the international demand by humans for shark products: fins, liver oil (used to waterproof wooden boats), skin and meat. Whale Sharks continue to be hunted in parts of Asia, such as the Philippines. They are also impacted indirectly by fisheries, becoming entangled in nets and being hit by fishing vessels.

Whale Sharks are solitary creatures. Although massive, they are docile and will sometimes allow swimmers to hitch a ride. Parts of their skin are incredibly tough and covered in hard, tooth-like scales called denticles; the hide on a Whale Shark's back can be up to 10 centimetres (4 inches) thick. Conversely, their underbellies are relatively soft and vulnerable, so when approached by divers a Whale Shark will often turn its belly away from them.

Diving with these gentle giants has become a very popular tourism activity over the last twenty years. This kind of ecotourism is a double-edged sword. On the one hand, the increase in boating activities and close approaches by divers can interfere with the behaviour and feeding of the Whale Sharks. On the other, it brings increased attention for the need to study and protect these mysterious creatures, which is a positive outcome. Conservation groups are working with tour operators to raise awareness of Whale Shark behaviour and to promote safer diving and boating practices that will reduce any negative impacts upon the Whale Sharks.

Whale Shark cruising in the Maldives.

Opposite: A Whale Shark
filter feeding — dangerous
only to plankton!

Below: A Whale Shark
accompanied by remora fish.

Tour boats with swimmers and a Whale Shark in Holbox, Mexico.

Whale Sharks and communities

Jackie Ziegler, Environmental Social Scientist

My research focuses on the conservation value of marine ecotourism. I am interested in understanding whether working in community-based ecotourism can lead to greater support for conservation of both the focal species, like Whale Sharks, and the wider marine environment.

WHY DO YOU DO WHAT YOU DO?

I fell in love with the ocean as a child when snorkelling in Florida and Hawaii. Consequently, I did my undergraduate studies in marine biology, but I quickly transitioned to marine social science after I realized that conservation issues are actually a people issue!

WHAT DO YOU THINK IS THE PUBLIC APPEAL OF YOUR ANIMAL?

Whale Sharks are not what you would expect a shark to look like. They're big, with a spot pattern that looks like an underwater constellation. Yet they have no teeth, at least not the teeth you would expect from a shark. Swimming with them is a truly special, once-in-a-lifetime experience.

WHAT HAVE BEEN YOUR BIGGEST LESSONS LEARNT?

The main lesson I've learnt is that conservation is not an environmental issue, it is a people issue. Therefore, understanding why humans behave the way we do is critical to address environmental problems.

WHAT ARE YOUR 'STRATEGIES OF HOPE' FOR CONSERVATION?

Although conservation is a global issue, conservation success is best achieved at the local level. Conservation can't be implemented by science in a vacuum. Science must be partnered with the local communities that share the ecosystems. We must work with local communities and include them in the conservation process in a just and equitable way. It is vital that we listen to the needs of local communities and ensure that any conservation approaches will match their needs. Communities must feel they have ownership of their ecosystem in order for conservation of those ecosystems to be successful.

WHAT ARE YOUR HOPES FOR THE FUTURE?

My hope for the future is that we can shift the perceptions people have towards sharks, from dangerous killing machines to one of respect. Whale Sharks, I believe, can play a key role in that shift as they are an ideal species to get people caring about sharks, so that sharks are not just seen as man-eating machines, but are viewed as an integral part of the ocean ecosystem. Whale Sharks, as a charismatic species, can rally community support for conservation of the entire ecosystem of which communities are a part.

A swimmer shadows a Whale Shark.

A New Zealand Kākā
with its distinctly
curved beak and rich
colouration.

CHAPTER 13

Kākā

It is hard to argue against the proposition that penguins are the cornerstone of charisma in the bird world, but amongst flying birds the charisma police would probably identify parrots as the most likely suspects. Parrots have character in abundance and New Zealand's endangered **Kākā** is amongst the most characterful of them all. A large olive-green and brown coloured bird, standing 46 centimetres (18 inches) tall, with scarlet underwings, cheeks that grade subtly from orange to red, and a crimson belly, Kākā are pretty snappy dressers too.

Their most striking characteristics, however, are their large, hooked beaks, which look more like talons, and their propensity for making noise. They are generally heard before they are seen, calling raucously high up in the forests. They gather in large flocks, especially in the early morning and late evening, making such a racket and generally being so boisterous that the indigenous Māori believed they were gossiping.

Kākā have been in decline ever since the arrival of Europeans to New Zealand, especially from the nineteenth century onwards. There are estimated to be only about 10,000 Kākā remaining. Despite their widespread distribution throughout New Zealand, the populations of Kākā have been hammered due to forest clearance and predation by introduced mammals. Offshore islands that are free of stoats — such as Kapiti, Little Barrier, Great Barrier, Hen, Stewart, Mayor, Codfish, and Ulva Islands — are their best sanctuary at the moment. Having evolved in the absence of mammalian predators, the lifestyle of Kākā makes them easy prey: they nest deep in hollow trees from which there is no escape if they get hunted by stoats, rats and possums that eat their eggs and chicks; the young leave the nest before they can fly; and incubating females are easily attacked and killed by stoats. Male Kākā do not contribute to incubation duties and, as a consequence, there are now more males than females left in the population.

Kākā have a sweet tooth and feed on nectar, fruit and seeds found largely in the canopy of the forest. Kākā also eat honeydew, which is excreted by scale insects from the bark of beech trees. The sugary food is an important part of the Kākā's diet and, indeed, may be essential for it to breed in beech forests — although the birds now have competition for the sweet, sticky liquid from introduced wasps. Kākā also wield their strong beaks to good effect, tearing strips of bark from trees to look for insects and to access the trees' sap.

Kākā breed for the first time when they are around three years old. The female lays a clutch of typically four eggs, which are incubated for three weeks until they hatch. The grey,

A Kākā feeds on a flax bush.

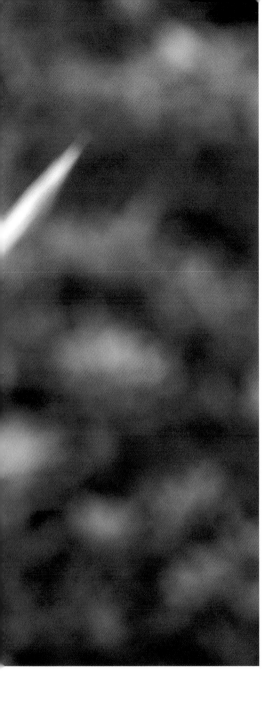

A Kākā's talons mirror its bill, enabling it to hang on upside down.

The cheeks of the Kākā are mottled orange and olive-green.

Kākā look alike, so scientists use leg bands to identify them.

down-covered chicks remain in the nest for ten weeks until they fledge, feathered but flightless, and ever so noisy. They have to spend up to a week on the ground before their feathers are developed enough for flight. All up, it takes a Kākā over three months from go to whoa; from newly-laid egg to newly-airborne youngster. That is an awfully long time to be stuck either on the ground or in the trees and, therefore, exposed to predators such as stoats.

The future of Kākā depends upon controlling or eliminating introduced mammalian predators from New Zealand's forests. Translocation programs that reintroduce Kākā to areas where stoats, possums and rats have been eradicated have proven remarkably successful. But if these playful parrots are to return to their former copious and cacophonous glory in the forests throughout New Zealand, it will require educating the public about the need for conservation and enlisting their help.

A Kākā at a feeding station uses its feet in lieu of hands.

CASE STUDY

Kākā as ambassadors for conservation

Tahu Mackenzie, Environmental Educator

I have been lucky enough to work as the education officer at New Zealand's Orokonui Ecosanctuary for the last eleven years, working with my favourite native bird, the Kākā. Orokonui Ecosanctuary is a 307-hectare community-led restoration project and a protected paradise for our native flora and fauna, encircled by a 9.5-kilometre (6-mile) predator-resistant fence. We opened to the public in 2007 and translocated six Kākā that year. These charismatic birds had been extinct locally for 130 years. We now have a population of more than 50 birds.

WHY DO YOU DO WHAT YOU DO?

I was so lucky to grow up surrounded by nature until I turned seven, when I moved with my mother, an academic, to live in a number of large cities abroad. This encouraged me to think and feel ecologically and to dedicate my life to serving the real world, the natural world. I was fortunate to train in the performing arts to communicate stories of the natural world. I came on board at Orokonui Ecosanctuary as education officer in 2009, and work with more than 10,000 students every year, from early childhood, primary, secondary, tertiary and community education groups.

WHAT DO YOU THINK IS THE PUBLIC APPEAL OF YOUR ANIMAL?

South Island Kākā are my favourite native birds, with the perfect combination of qualities to engage humans with their plight as an endangered species. Stunningly beautiful, highly intelligent and endemic to New Zealand, Kākā were the mōkai rangatira, the most chiefly companion birds of Māori. They have a tendency to be friendly, sociable and playful with humans. The Kākā has become the mascot of community conservation projects in Dunedin, with the community embracing this iconic native species creatively in murals, window decorations and costumes at local events.

WHAT HAVE BEEN YOUR BIGGEST LESSONS LEARNT?

We need the whole community to help us protect the Kākā and the ecosanctuary! The best way I have found to engage with the public is to give them memorable and emotionally nourishing educational experiences that they will associate with Orokonui. These experiences don't have to take part at Orokonui to be effective, as long as the association is there. I went to a large hardware store and a shopping mall in the city centre, both venues where I could access large groups of people for fun workshops that connected them with nature in their own backyards (e.g. by making birdfeeders). In this way, I raised awareness for Orokonui and empowered families and the public to feel they could make a difference.

WHAT ARE YOUR 'STRATEGIES OF HOPE' FOR CONSERVATION?

Hands-on, fun, educational experiences and citizen science have proved really powerful. I see creative eco-technology as a central strategy of hope for conservation. My partner and I invented birdfeeders that enable the monitoring of native bird populations using cameras in people's backyards while also protecting the native birds from cats by giving them 360 degrees of visibility while they feed. If native birdfeeding and introduced predator trapping become part of our daily lives as New Zealanders, we can ensure a safe future for our precious native species, which are not found anywhere else in the world and are at risk of extinction.

WHAT ARE YOUR HOPES FOR THE FUTURE?

My hopes for the future are that we all come to recognize ourselves as the triumph of nature's art, that we are here to make things better for all life. We have recently received funding to carry out community engagement and radio tracking of our Kākā at Orokonui. This gives me great hope as we will be able to find out so much more about the adventures our precious Kākā are having inside and outside the ecosanctuary. We can also use this research to bring to life for the whole community what they can do every day to help the Kākā.

Tahu showing a Kākā to school children at Orokonui Ecosanctuary near Dunedin, New Zealand.

Monarch Butterflies

Charisma comes in all sizes. In the insect realm, when it comes to charisma, **Monarch Butterflies** reign supreme. Their handsome colouration and complex long-distance migrations are mesmerizing. Each year, millions of Monarch Butterflies undertake what must be the most incredible migration in all the animal kingdom.

The Monarch Butterfly is instantly recognizable with its orange wings, which are laced with black lines and bordered with white dots. Its colourful paint job makes it easy to identify and, really, that's its purpose: the bright colours serve as a warning to predators that this butterfly is poisonous and they should not risk attacking it. The poison comes from their food — milkweed. Milkweed is toxic but Monarch Butterflies have

Monarch Butterflies in the oyamel fir trees of their overwintering ground in Mexico.

Millions of Monarch Butterflies give the evergreen fir trees the appearance of being deciduous trees with autumn leaves.

The Monarchs cluster
together tightly like
lepidopteran pine cones.

The distinctly patterned Monarch Butterfly clinging to milkweed.

evolved to not only tolerate it, but to use its toxicity to their advantage. The adult female Monarch Butterfly lays tiny eggs covered with a sticky substance on the underside of the poisonous milkweed leaves. The caterpillar hatches from its egg several days later and munches on the milkweed leaves. When ten to fourteen days old, the caterpillar goes into its pupa stage, where it is encased in a jade green chrysalis. During the next ten to fourteen days, a miraculous transformation takes place and it metamorphoses from plump, awkward caterpillar to an elegant and ephemeral adult butterfly. Both the caterpillar and adult butterfly store the poison from the milkweed in their bodies as a deterrent to protect them from being eaten. And Monarch Butterflies deserve all the protection they can get. Not only are some birds, like orioles, able to stomach the poison and eat the adult butterflies, but other insects like wasps and ants could prey on the caterpillars, which are also vulnerable to spiders. Yet it is the migration of the Monarchs that puts them most in jeopardy.

Each spring, Monarch Butterflies migrate north from their wintering grounds in Mexico, following a 'milkweed highway' to the northern parts of the Unites States and Canada — a journey of up to 4800 kilometres (3000 miles)! Except that they don't do it all in one go as individuals: they complete the journey through their offspring and their offspring's offspring. It might take as many as five generations of the butterflies to complete the northwards migration, as first one lot stops after a few

hundred miles to breed on patches of milkweed (and then promptly dies — the average life span of a Monarch Butterfly on the northward route is only five to seven weeks) and, when the next generation of butterflies emerge from their chrysalises, they fly a bit further north, find some milkweed, and then repeat the process. Because the seasons are later the further the butterflies move north, they are essentially tracking the blooming of their food source, the various species of milkweed. By early autumn, it is starting to turn cold in the north and a new 'Super Butterfly' generation of hardy and long-lived Monarch Butterflies turns south and migrates all the way back to their wintering colonies in Mexico and California all by themselves, travelling up to 160 kilometres (100 miles) per day. This generation of butterflies lives for about eight months, with the ones in Mexico huddling together during the winter in the tops of oyamel fir tree forests on the sides of mountains at nearly 3.2 kilometres (2 miles) above sea level. Come spring, they fly a little north to places like Texas, mate and lay their eggs on milkweed, and the whole multigenerational migration begins again.

It's not at all clear how they do this. They can take directional cues from the sun, they're responsive to the dying back of the milkweed, and they are sensitive to temperatures. But those are just small pieces of a much bigger puzzle. Bird migration has long fascinated scientists — how can a fledgling gannet, for example, taking its first ever flight from Cape Kidnappers in New Zealand, fly unassisted and by itself to Australia?

Right: Monarchs overwinter in Mexico in the tops of oyamel fir trees at over 3 kilometres (nearly 2 miles) above sea level.

Above: A Monarch Butterfly pupa hangs from a stem of milkweed as the caterpillar metamorphoses into an adult butterfly.

The best, if still incomplete, answer is that the birds are hard-wired; it's something determined by their genes. But if that beggars belief, then how to explain the multigenerational migration of Monarch Butterflies in North America, where each generation seems programmed to do something different? And such a feat of endurance, too, for something as small and fragile as a butterfly.

Unfortunately, these super creatures are declining rapidly due to decreasing food sources (i.e. the milkweed on which the Monarch caterpillars depend) resulting from modern farming practices and urbanization, along with the loss of overwintering habitats in Mexico from logging. Broad-spectrum insecticides used in agriculture and household gardens kill many Monarch Butterflies every year. Climate change, too, is almost certainly taking its toll because this insect's lifecycle is so attuned to temperatures and the changing of the seasons.

On the positive side, concerns for this charismatic microfauna have resulted in the designation of protected areas in Mexico and tri-national conservation strategies between Canada, Mexico and the United States. The Monarch Butterfly Biosphere Reserve in Mexico has, since its establishment in the 1980s, attracted millions of visitors from around the world.

A line of Monarch
Butterflies 'nose to tail'.

CASE STUDY

Monarchs, migration and milkweed

Harvey Lemelin, Social Scientist

While we know quite a bit about Monarch Butterflies, we know very little of the tourists who come to see them every year or how tourism contributes to the conservation of these animals and the betterment of the surrounding communities. My goal has been to contribute to a greater understanding of Monarch Butterfly tourism. The more we learn of these fascinating animals, the more we can educate people, preserve the required habitat and conserve these magnificent butterflies.

Left: The Monarch
Butterflies in Mexico
have become a major
tourist attraction.

WHY DO YOU DO WHAT YOU DO?
Because insects are fascinating! While not the only insect to migrate, the migration of Monarch Butterflies is one of the longest and most spectacular in the world. Indeed, what makes this migration so fascinating is that the northward journey from Mexico to Canada and the United States is multigenerational, meaning that it takes two to four generations of Monarchs to make the journey back to Canada, where I live. Then in the late summer totally different generations of the Monarch Butterfly will fly all the way from Canada to Mexico, overwinter in the Sierra Madres, mate and lay their eggs, and prepare the next generation for the northward journey. That's pretty amazing!

WHAT DO YOU THINK IS THE PUBLIC APPEAL OF YOUR ANIMAL?
Images of butterflies can be found on the ancient pyramids

Right: Tree tops are no barrier for a creature that can fly thousands of kilometres and reach great altitudes.

of San Juan, Teotihuacan, and Tulum in Mexico. Butterflies and have inspired artists, jewellers and potters, and are incorporated into various Hopi, Toltec, Mayan, Aztec and other Indigenous peoples' legends across North America.

The popularity of Monarch Butterflies is not that surprising. Easily recognizable and prevalent throughout North America, Monarch Butterflies are often welcomed into people's gardens. In fact, people will deliberately transform their yards by planting milkweed and other flowers just for Monarchs. Others will participate in citizen science projects just for the opportunity to view and interact with these animals. Tourists will travel hundreds and sometimes thousands of miles just to witness the congregations of millions of Monarchs in Mexico. As someone who has had the opportunity to do all three, I can attest to the charisma and appeal of this microfauna.

WHAT HAVE BEEN YOUR BIGGEST LESSONS LEARNT?

Butterflies are often described as 'gentle creatures' embodying kindness and mildness. What I have come to realize is that you don't survive a migration of several thousands of kilometres by being 'gentle' — you survive by being persistent and resilient, overcoming harsh climate fluctuations, predators, cities and various other obstacles. If we give these animals a chance by preserving their overwintering colonies in Mexico and providing them with food and nursery plants along their travels, then they will find a way to survive. We have a responsibility to play in the conservation and preservation of these magnificent creatures.

WHAT ARE YOUR 'STRATEGIES OF HOPE' FOR CONSERVATION?

The various tri-lateral agreements and cooperative management strategies surrounding Monarch Butterflies suggest that governmental agencies and various other partners in North America can work together to protect and conserve a truly iconic species. One of the fundamental components of these conservation strategies is tourism. Tourism showcasing wildlife such as Monarch Butterflies should promote respect in tourists and generate income and empowerment for local communities. It is a symbiotic relationship, with an understanding that without the attraction (the Monarchs) there can be no tourism. Hence, it is essential that we preserve and protect the butterflies and their habitat.

WHAT ARE YOUR HOPES FOR THE FUTURE?

Being a multigenerational migration (at least for the northward journey), the Monarch Butterfly migration forces us to see habitat protection and animal conservation through much different lenses. What we need to realize is that while the protection of the overwintering grounds in Mexico is crucial, the implementation of a 'milkweed way' consisting of milkweed plants throughout the North American continent is also essential to the wellbeing of Monarch Butterflies. Only by taking such steps can we help ensure that this amazing animal will continue its migration throughout North America.

My goal as a researcher is to remind people of that and to also remind them that we have inherited this planet from seven generations in the future. Therefore, we must strive to leave this place in a condition such that in seven generations from now, millions of Monarch Butterflies will still undertake their journeys and our descendants will able to witness and enjoy this amazing phenomenon themselves.

CHAPTER 15

Great Apes

When you look into the eyes of an ape you see an intelligent, self-aware animal looking back at you. Appraising you. We don't just descend from apes: we are apes. Humans are part of the Great Ape family and our evolutionary brothers and sisters are Chimpanzees, Bonobos, Orangutans and Gorillas. We recognize their emotions as similar to our own. They are strong but gentle. They are patently smart: they use tools and can copy behaviour by observing it in others. These similarities make it easy for humans to anthropomorphize Great Apes.

Great Apes are named for their large bodies. Notably, they also have larger brains than other primates. We share the majority of our genetic material with Great Apes. Like us, they make and use tools, work together and form social groups in which they share and help others, even laughing with one another. They have strong family groups and distinct cultures. Great Apes have their own language of gestures,

An adult Chimpanzee pauses to listen to the distant calls of another Chimpanzee troupe. Uganda.

A silverback Mountain Gorilla keeps a watchful and protective eye over his family in the mountain jungle forests of Bwindi National Park, Uganda.

Left: High in the forest canopy, an adult Chimpanzee fixes his gaze upon the photographer and vice versa. Uganda.

similar to sign language or body language. They can pick up language just like human children do: by watching, listening and trying it out for themselves. Great Apes experience emotions and desires.

Great Apes live in Africa and Asia and tend to live in jungles, mountainous areas and savannas. Apes have offspring much like humans: giving birth to one or two babies at a time after a gestation period of around nine months. They breastfeed their young and take care of them for many years. For some species it can take twelve to eighteen years for the offspring to fully develop into an adult. Many ape species are endangered — due to human pressure on their natural environment, being killed for bushmeat, or captured in the wild in the name of the illegal ape trade. They are exploited in zoos, circuses and amusement parks, and bought as pets.

Great Apes can live for a long time. **Chimpanzees** can live up to 50 years in the wild. Chimps warn their friends of danger and even wage war over territory and kill one another. Social learning is common in chimps. They learn to make tools from one another. They will eat just about anything. For a long time, we assumed they were herbivores, but it turns out that Chimpanzees are omnivores, meaning they eat both meat and plants. They use sticks to extract termites from their nests and they

Portrait of a female Orangutan.

Left: A baby Orangutan cradled by its mother.

Below: An elder Chimpanzee has climbed down from the tree branches to the forest floor to rest in the cool shade of the trees. Uganda.

Opposite: The beautiful hazel-coloured eyes of a silverback Mountain Gorilla.

eat the meat of monkeys, in particular the Red Colobus monkey. Chimpanzees make a new nest for sleeping every day. In fact, their beds are less likely to harbour bacteria compared to human beds because of this daily rebuilding habit.

Orangutans are the world's largest tree-dwelling animal. They have the most intense relationship between mother and young of any non-human mammal. For the first eight years of a young Orangutan's life, its mother is its constant companion. Until another baby is born, mothers sleep in a nest with their offspring every night. The main threat to the survival of wild Orangutan populations is the massive destruction of tropical rainforests in Borneo and Sumatra fuelled by the global demand for palm oil.

Gorillas live in complex social groups, display individual personalities, make and use tools, and show emotions like grief and compassion. They use a range of complex vocalizations to communicate information in different contexts and are even capable of learning basic human sign language. Mountain Gorillas are an endangered species, living in just two forests in central Africa: Bwindi and Virunga. Since they do not survive in captivity, the only conservation effort possible for the species is nature-based tourism — tourists visit wild habituated Gorillas, ensuring the necessary capital to protect the habitat.

Despite the growing number of tourists visiting Mountain Gorillas and an increasing number of habituated groups, very little data has been collected on the potential impacts of tourism on the behaviour of the Gorillas.

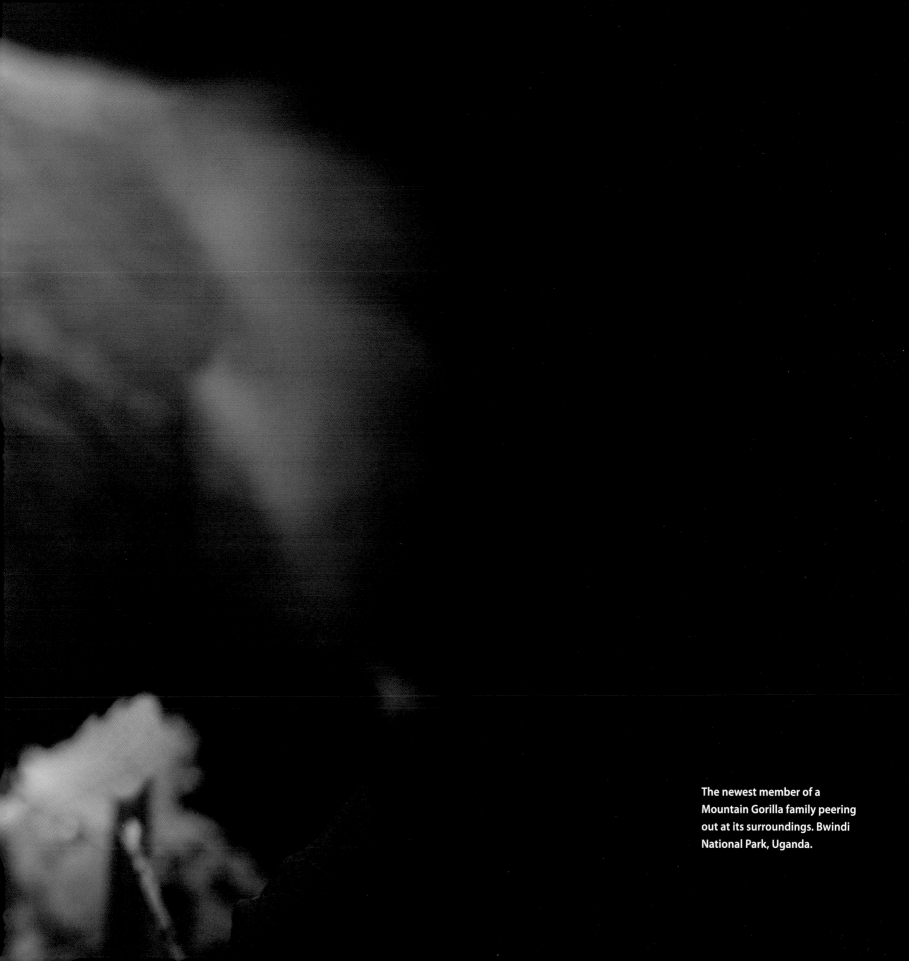

The newest member of a
Mountain Gorilla family peering
out at its surroundings. Bwindi
National Park, Uganda.

WHY DO YOU DO WHAT YOU DO?

I always wanted to know what animals were thinking. During my college years, I was introduced to ethology and found in it a way to get inside the minds of animals. I became interested in Mountain Gorillas, but no zoo in the world houses this species. Moreover, the wild population was declining so rapidly that the species was feared to become extinct by the end of the twentieth century. It did not. Instead, in the past decade, the Mountain Gorilla population has more than doubled! One important driver for its recovery has been nature-based tourism. By bringing tourists (and capital) to visit Gorillas, we ensure the protection of their habitat and the generation of local employment. But how do Gorillas feel about our presence? Is it good or bad for them? We do know that wild animals react to people in different ways: approaching,

CASE STUDY

Mountain Gorillas and tourism in Uganda

Raquel Costa, Primatologist

My work aims to examine how interactions with human tourists influence Mountain Gorilla behaviour in Bwindi Impenetrable National Park, Uganda. This information will help the local authorities to develop management plans for Gorilla tourism that focus on minimizing disturbance levels for the animals, helping refine tourist education regarding their own behaviour in front of Gorillas in order to promote the animals' typical calm behaviour. This aims to reduce the potential risks of conflicts as well as building the visitors' sense of responsibility to enhance sustainable tourism.

avoiding, attacking and ignoring. But it is less clear if this entails any stress or social disturbance for the animals. Maintaining the animals' welfare is not just the ethical thing to do, it is also a necessity to keep nature-based tourism sustainable and contribute to the conservation of healthy Mountain Gorillas for many years to come.

WHAT DO YOU THINK IS THE PUBLIC APPEAL OF YOUR ANIMAL?

Movies like *King Kong* and *Gorillas in the Mist* have helped to create a mystical view of gorillas. They are one of the strongest animals alive — they could easily kill you — but they have a shy and gentle nature. There is an appeal to get to know them better. Moreover, being one of our closest relatives, we see ourselves projected in them. For example, gorillas' family units come together to protect their infants as their primary function, which is also one of our society's core functions.

WHAT HAVE BEEN YOUR BIGGEST LESSONS LEARNT?

I was touched by the mutual respect between wild animals and local people walking side by side in Bwindi. I do believe that this respect was one of the major factors allowing the peaceful coexistence between both and, ultimately, the prosperity of nature-based tourism in the region. On the other hand, I have seen tourists' complete lack of respect for the established safe distance rules to be kept from the animals (7-metre/23-feet minimal distance for their safety and ours …). The risks of close association with tourists — who could bring new pathogens for which the Gorillas have no immunity — are severe. Examples of this direct threat to the Gorillas' health were sadly verified in the past, with reported lethal cases of infectious human-origin respiratory disease outbreaks in Gorillas.

WHAT ARE YOUR 'STRATEGIES OF HOPE' FOR CONSERVATION?

Any conservation action will only work if the local community is involved, to effectively implement conservation management plans. In Bwindi, the local governments have created the mechanisms to overcome damage to local fauna and flora by using Gorillas to attract enough capital to protect the park. Nevertheless, continuous monitoring is necessary to ensure the Gorillas' welfare and health while also promoting public education. A peaceful and respectful coexistence of all parties (Gorillas, local population and tourists) with shared benefits between wildlife and humans is possible.

WHAT ARE YOUR HOPES FOR THE FUTURE?

Each one of us has the potential to become a conservationist. Tragic images — forests being burned, animals succumbing to trash we throw into the oceans — enter our screens by the hour. However, when facing so many disasters, we need positive examples to inspire and motivate us. Nature-based tourism, while still being refined for Mountain Gorillas, has already proven to have positive outcomes for the Gorillas and local communities. We need to ensure a fair distribution of benefits for both animals and humans.

An attentive Gorilla mother tenderly grooms her young baby. Uganda.

CHAPTER 16

Wildlife selfies and sustainable tourism

Chapter co-written with Philip Seddon

Most of us love to travel and watch wildlife, but in a world of mass tourism the question is, are we in danger of doing more harm than good? Research shows that things can get out of hand quickly: if you are feeding wild animals, you might be killing them with kindness; and in trying to get an up-close encounter with wild animals you could be causing them distress. After all, we all need our personal space.

A free diver witnesses a pod of Sperm Whales resting in their unique vertical floating position. Dominica.

A Great White Shark enthusiast poses for a selfie with his favourite animal. Guadalupe Island, Mexico.

One of the key challenges for management of human–wildlife encounters is that most of the impacts on wildlife are hard to see for the untrained eye and, moreover, they are incremental and cumulative. In other words, while attempting to capture our own special moments encountering wildlife, we might be contributing to a species' demise through impacts that are largely out of sight and, therefore, out of mind.

The photos in this book are a testament to the power of images — how can you not rejoice in seeing such gorgeous creatures? Our human desire to connect with nature, combined with today's ubiquity and ease of use of technology capable of capturing and sharing photos on social media, has given rise to a phenomenon of 'wildlife selfies', self-portraits taken with an animal in the frame or even in hand. Whether it's swimming with dolphins, feeding monkeys, patting a tiger or riding an elephant, our

compulsion to get close to wildlife and to snap, post and share wildlife selfies is contributing to the exploitation of many charismatic animals, often to their detriment.

In New Zealand, few wildlife species are as attractive or as accessible to the public as penguins. Close human proximity for many penguin species is known to reduce their biological fitness, by causing stress and disrupting normal behaviours such as feeding, mating and chick-rearing. **Hoiho**, New Zealand's unique and endangered Yellow-eyed Penguin, is known to be one of the penguin species that is most sensitive to human disturbance, yet small breeding populations persist only a short drive from major urban areas. Research has shown that Hoiho breeding

in areas with unregulated human access have lower breeding success.

Wildlife selfies can occur in a range of settings, from wild to captive settings, where animals may or may not have a choice in the interaction — or even in situations where wild animals are being caught and handled for legitimate research or management purposes. Often the context of any such images will be unclear, particularly where the focus of the human subject is on the camera. Social media platforms provide a simple means to publish such photos, which can be for a range of purposes, from the socially well-motivated (e.g. raising awareness and support for wildlife conservation) through to the vainglorious and less well-motivated (e.g. crafting one's public image of an amazing personal life and encounters with exotic wild animals). This can all create a distorted perception that wild animals are there to be approached, handled and photographed.

Ecotourists position themselves for a good look at a wild Chimpanzee as he goes about his day. Uganda.

This has led to an increase in people, for example, seeking their own wildlife selfies with Hoiho and, in the most extreme cases, people chasing and trying to capture penguins on the beach or following them inland to their nest sites. Faced with ongoing threats from fisheries, exotic predators and climate change, human disturbance is like the final nail in the coffin, one that is driving mainland Hoiho populations to extinction.

Biophilic tendencies mean that humans are generally drawn towards nature, and encounters with wildlife can engender a sense of awe, concern and stewardship that can translate into concrete support for conservation. On the other hand, we could be 'loving them to death' if our interactions with wildlife cause stress to animals, thereby reducing survival, breeding and overall population fitness. Our Instagram profile can say a lot about us so let's make sure it does not say 'I'm an idiot': take pictures of wildlife and talk about your experiences online but do it from an appropriate distance and provide context. Love equals respect.

Can wildlife selfies be used for good? Social media platforms and social media influencers can act to reduce harmful impacts of inappropriate wildlife selfies. A *good* wildlife selfie is a picture where there is no contact between an animal and a human, and the animal is not being restrained or held in captivity to be a used as a photo prop, but is clearly free to stay or to move. Such appropriate wildlife selfies can raise awareness

Top to bottom: A diver takes a selfie with a Seadragon; Kayakers taking selfies with a feeding Humpback Whale in Monterey Bay, USA; Visitors observing Yellow-Eyed Penguins from a viewing hide on Otago Peninsula, New Zealand; Adult Yellow-Eyed Penguin with chick on Otago Peninsula, New Zealand.

for conservation efforts, if presented in context. Some key challenges remain but, if addressed, could create conservation wins for penguins and other wildlife by creating realistic visitor expectations for interactions with wildlife.

On a personal level we need to question whether our connection with nature requires us to be inserted into animals' lives and to be aware of the often-severe consequences we can have for the animals. Mindfulness, empathy and putting ourselves into another creature's position are a good starting point. Clearly, managing visitor expectations is a critical task for wildlife tourism. Here, only informed, caring and empowered members of the public can make responsible consumer choices by choosing ethical wildlife tour operators and well-managed recreational wildlife encounters.

More effective science communication can help inform people of the benefits, risks and other costs of their decisions. Marketing of responsible wildlife viewing practices can provide a sustainable and environment-friendly edge and can even create a competitive advantage for such operators. This would lead to satisfied visitors who understand that best-practice viewing behaviour and respecting proximity regulations are in the best interests of wildlife. A sustainable tourism operation based upon the welfare and long-term conservation of wildlife can then become the foundation for successful business operations. Sustainable tourism management in one of the most remote places on Earth may well hold the answer.

Left: A first-time visitor to Antarctica is thrilled to be among a colony of Rockhopper Penguins.

Visitors to Antarctica get a front-row view as a Humpback Whale feeds on zooplankton.

Antarctic tourism

Thomas Bauer, Polar Expedition Guide/ Sustainable Tourism Researcher

My research into Antarctic tourism began in 1991 when I started my PhD in the Department of Geography and Environmental Science at Monash University in Melbourne, Australia. In the early 1990s, very little was known about tourism activities and their impacts in Antarctica. I set out to investigate first-hand and, at last count, I have participated in 35 Antarctic voyages as an expedition guide, lecturer and Zodiac driver. Based on my observations, I can say that Antarctic tourism is the best managed tourism in the world.

WHY DO YOU DO WHAT YOU DO?

I keep going back to Antarctica every year to continue to observe how tourism is conducted. In particular I am there to guide visitors ashore to ensure they enjoy the penguin encounters without getting too close. A minimum distance of 5 metres (16½ feet) has to be maintained between humans and penguins. At times, visitors are so excited while ashore that they try to get too close to the wildlife and my colleagues and I are there to gently remind them of the distance they have to keep.

WHAT DO YOU THINK IS THE PUBLIC APPEAL OF YOUR ANIMAL?

Penguins are the signature animals of Antarctica and visitors enjoy watching them going about their routines such as courtship, mating, sitting on eggs or feeding their young. Yes, penguins are considered cute animals but more importantly they are incredibly tough creatures that are extremely well adapted to the climatic conditions in which they live. They are marine animals that spend most of their life in the freezing waters surrounding Antarctica and they only come on land to breed and to raise their chicks. On the island of South Georgia in the South Atlantic, visitors have the opportunity to visit King Penguin colonies that number over 100,000 birds, an unforgettable experience where penguins often approach visitors.

Emperor Penguins trek across their frigid and starkly beautiful Antarctic domain.

A Zodiac point of view of the mirror-like fjords of Svalbard, Norway.

WHAT HAVE BEEN YOUR BIGGEST LESSONS LEARNT?

My greatest challenge as an Antarctic researcher was to get to the continent to experience how tourism was being conducted. I became part of the multi-year Project Antarctic Conservation at the Scott Polar Research Institute of Cambridge University, and this allowed me to participate in my first voyage south in 1994.

The biggest lesson learnt is that tourism in the greatest wilderness on the planet is being conducted in such a way that no harm is being done to the Antarctic environment and that tourist visits have no more than a transitory impact on places visited. As expedition guides, we have to pass annual tests, visitors have to attend compulsory briefings on how to behave while ashore, and biosecurity measures such as boot washing before and after landings are mandatory to protect landing sites.

WHAT ARE YOUR 'STRATEGIES OF HOPE' FOR CONSERVATION?

There is much talk about environmental sustainability but there is not enough action. I try to be different and, after years of exposure to the beauty and largely untouched nature of Antarctica, I decided it was time to put my money where my mouth is. As a consequence, in 2002 my family bought a 15-hectare (38-acre) lowland rainforest near Mission Beach in Queensland that had been identified as critical cassowary habitat. We placed a conservation covenant on the land that protects the forest forever. My hope is that other people will follow suit, buying land to protect it rather than to exploit it. I understand that not everyone has the means to buy land but at the very minimum everyone can play a role in conservation by taking a good look at their lifestyle practices and adjusting them in such a way that they minimize negative impacts on the environment. Aboard ship in the polar regions, I give a lecture entitled 'From the ice to the rainforest: From words to action' in which I encourage people to do what they can to make positive contributions to environmental protection and conservation.

WHAT ARE YOUR HOPES FOR THE FUTURE?

My hope is that Antarctica will continue to be the best managed tourism destination in the world and that other tourism destinations learn from the way tourism is conducted in the south. From a global perspective, my hope is that humanity wakes up to the fact that we are damaging our small planet and that people should adjust their lives to minimize the negative impacts they are having on their environments.

A hopeful ending

The previous chapters have highlighted a variety of conservation projects in different parts of the world, centred around charismatic wildlife that represent a combination of beauty, awe, danger, endangerment, cuteness and rareness.

Undoubtedly, charisma and cute appeal have the power to capture the imagination of the public and serve as a leverage for environmental action and regulations. However, this bias can also result in reduced conservation awareness for species perceived as less charismatic. It is, therefore, important to remember that there are many other species sharing our planet that require conservation attention and protection.

Research shows that our human desire to connect with nature can create problems for wildlife around the world, especially if we express the awe we feel by trying to get physically close to, and even touch, wildlife. This adoration can cause significant negative, even fatal, impacts on wildlife that can be hard to see. Here, science communication and responsible marketing can increase awareness about such impacts, promote responsible practices, and provide relevant context to the public. At the same time we need to leverage our human affinity for wildlife, maximize educational and conservation benefits, and celebrate the good that is possible.

As a young girl I dreamt of becoming a scientist and changing the world. Forty years later, I recognize that the world has changed me instead: I see it now as a canvas that consists of intriguing shades of grey rather than a world that once seemed so black and white. I have learnt to value the power of communication, of people and of resilience. I remain, like my young self in the forests and backyards of my childhood, full of awe, wonder and hope. While there are many challenges when it comes to conservation projects around the world, a feeling of hopefulness can make a real difference. Hope-based communication is a simple way to focus on promoting the values and solutions we want to see in society. It creates a climate of togetherness, empathy, and taking responsibility to care for one another. In other words, when we believe that we can exercise some control over a particular situation, we are empowered to make a difference and feel that our contributions are desired and valued.

Researchers describe a prominent culture of hopelessness amongst scientists, who often spend their days modelling how quickly their favourite species will disappear — in a sense, writing obituaries for nature. While despair about the planet has many labels, increasingly conservationists are starting to worry that their message is counterproductive. The doom-and-gloom niche in science is oversubscribed, and its message will likely resonate with only a small proportion of the public that it is trying to spur to action. Research shows that appealing to our

A young islander from the
remote islands of Micronesia
proudly shows his find of the day:
newborn sea turtle hatchlings.

fears to spur conservation action by-and-large does not work: if an issue appears too daunting and makes people feel powerless and hopeless, they can become apathetic and desensitized to the actual message. By contrast, the hope niche is relatively vacant: a veritable new landscape poised for being populated by a radiation of ever more hopeful scientists and communities.

To be clear: it is important to acknowledge existing environmental and conservation crises. However, it is even more important to promote the fact that human actions can and do make a difference. A narrative of demise offers little direction, but stories about positive outcomes, with information about how they are achieved, create an opportunity to repeat that same strategy. In essence, hope engenders conservation success and this success breeds more success. The 'broaden and build' theory of positive emotions suggests that positive emotions are more constructive in the long-term as they foster our thought–action repertoire and ability to develop solution-focused pathways. Here, encouraging positive emotions such as hope is a critical element for motivating behavioural change, because it induces people to look at different options and come up with new ideas and thoughts. Confident expectations for future success — hope — increase personal effort, while low expectations (i.e. a lack of hope) correlate with giving up. If people expect little improvement, they will invest little effort to achieve it.

Humans are storytelling animals, whether around the campfire or on social media. Story is central to what it means to be human.

Conservation marketing and storytelling

Wiebke Finkler,
Communicator/Filmmaker

I started my career as a marine biologist, who then discovered the power of filmmaking and science communication as a tool to engage audiences. My research now focuses on storytelling using strategic marketing communication for the purposes of environmental and social change. This includes sustainable resource management, conservation and human–wildlife interactions. I have a particular interest in how video campaigns, when combined with community-based social marketing approaches, can be used as a tool for environmental change, conservation and social impact. I believe that to address the 'wicked problems' of our times, we need to stop looking for perfect solutions and instead focus on workable solutions; solutions that consider the needs of different stakeholders through participation and value co-creation. Step up marketing!

WHY DO YOU DO WHAT YOU DO?

That is simple: because I believe in the goodness of people and our power to do good. Growing up in a tiny German village surrounded by forests, rivers and lakes I was captured by the natural world from an early age. To me, nature remains magic and full of imaginaries. Studying biology, graduating in marine science, and researching sustainable whale watching was a natural path. When I realized that conservation really is all about understanding people and influencing relevant behaviours, I added filmmaking into my life's toolbox as a creative and exciting way to communicate science and empower audiences. Filmmaking enables me to tap into my childhood experiences — a world which I experience first and foremost through visuals and sound.

WHAT DO YOU THINK IS THE PUBLIC APPEAL OF YOUR ANIMAL?

My 'animal' of choice is humans and how we can be a become better, more empathetic and mindful version of ourselves; a version that does good in the world and is a champion for species less powerful than us. My research tool of choice is visual media, using

Storytelling is a powerful tool for engaging audiences about science and can become a driver and simulator for action. Hope-based storytelling for conservation involves making some dramatic changes in our thinking: from problems to solutions, from threat to opportunity, from against to for, from victims to heroes, and from fear to hope. In traditional science storytelling, scientists tend to be portrayed as the heroes battling for conservation and providing protection for biodiversity. Therein may just lie one of the contributors for the paralysis of the people that science is trying to reach: it is the scientists who are perceived as the Earth's paramedics and the people see themselves as simply bystanders. If we want people to take conservation and environmental action, we must make people see themselves as saviours who have agency.

When it comes to conservation, we can learn a lot from an unlikely ally: marketing — the study of brands and how to persuade people to buy products and services and, therefore, influence their behaviour. Bearing in mind that conservation is all about influencing human behaviour, marketing and science communication can be a joint force for conservation. Marketing has a long history of influencing human behaviour and has developed techniques and processes, based on social science and social psychology, that can help create positive change. It is here that community-based conservation marketing initiatives can make a real difference, help promote hope-based science, and offer agency and power to the people.

video as a storytelling medium. With it, I undertake pragmatic cross-disciplinary action research that merges marketing with science communication and uses the power of visual storytelling.

WHAT HAVE BEEN YOUR BIGGEST LESSONS LEARNT?

Conservation is first and foremost about the relationships we can build with people rather than about the species we are trying to save. Effective conservation requires continuous interaction amongst scientists, managers and key stakeholders — a very different approach to just developing a snappy talk or pamphlet. In conservation, it is co-created and shared values through participation and inclusion that will win the day. Storytelling is a potentially powerful tool. All too often, however, traditional science storytelling pitches the science or scientists as the hero of its storytelling. This has led to science sitting on a pedestal, often far removed from the everyday contexts involving resource management and communities. Instead, I believe, we need to give power to the people and turn everyday people into the heroes of our storytelling. When it comes to the communication of science, we have to replace stories of hopelessness — where people are painted as villains and the source of all evil with respect to environmental crises — with stories of hope, where people have agency and participate in creating the solutions. In this scenario, science experts should become mentors, empowering everyday community heroes and heroines to contribute, drive and co-create value-driven conservation solutions.

WHAT ARE YOUR 'STRATEGIES OF HOPE' FOR CONSERVATION?

In a nutshell: focusing on solutions not problems. Being humble, transparent and collaborative. Engaging with people, communities and stakeholders. Building trust and relationships with people by listening to their views and concerns while sharing a cup of tea. Empowering people and communities as agents of positive change for conservation and sustainable development. Seeking workable solutions rather than perfect solutions. And finally, a stubborn belief in the power and goodness of people to want to do the right thing if they have the means of doing so.

WHAT ARE YOUR HOPES FOR THE FUTURE?

That every child can dare to dream, have access to a backyard to watch ladybirds and shelter amongst the branches of a tree. Connection to nature is the foundation of childhood dreams and a driver for so many of the stories shared by the people who contributed to this book — and beyond.

Credits

TEXT CREDITS

For their insight, research and contribution to the story vignettes of individual chapters, I would like to thank (in order of chapters): Yolanda Van Heezik, Katherina Audley, Klemens Pütz, Chantal Pagel, Jill Bueddefeld, Michelle Staedler, Scott Davis, Natalie Schmitt, Christina Geijer, Katie Rowe, Dorothy Lowekutuk, Fred Bercovitch, Marco Festa-Bianchet, Emily Hynes, Jackie Ziegler, Tahu Mackenzie, Harvey Lemelin, Raquel Costa, and Thomas Bauer.

For their insights, research and contribution as co-authors of individual chapters I would like to thank: Lloyd Spencer Davis (Chapter 2 and Chapter 11) and Philip Seddon (Chapter16). For overall book editing input I would like to thank Lloyd Spencer Davis.

PHOTO CREDITS

All photos © Scott Davis with the exception of those listed below.

Bio Wiebke top: Photo © Martina Sandkühler
Dedication page: Photo © Lewis Hendry
p.8: Photo © Andy Thompson
www.andythompsonphotographynz.co.nz
p.11 Photo © Barnabas Hertelendy on Unsplash
p.12: Photo © Philip Seddon
p.13: Photo © Casey Horner on Unsplash
p.17, 18 and 20 right: Photos © Jodi Frediani
p.20 top left and p.21: Photos © Whales of Guerrero
p.25 top right: Photo © Lloyd Davis
p.28 top: Photo © Dr Martin Bauert
p.28 bottom and p.29: Photos © Klemens Pütz
p.36 bottom: Photo © Sabrina Seeler
p.36 top: Photo © Chantal Pagel
p.39: Photo © clkraus on Shutterstock
p.46 top and bottom: Photos © Jill Bueddefeld
p.49 and p.50: Photos © mana5280 on Unsplash
p.51 top: Photo © Jim Capwell
p.51 bottom: Photo © Jodi Frediani
p.52: Photo provided by Michelle Staedler
p.53: Photo © Jim Capwell
p.71: Photo © Uriel Soberanes on Unsplash
p.72: Photo © Dibesh Karmacharya
p.73: Photo © Frida Bredesen on Unsplash
p.80 top: Photo provided by Christina Geijer
p.80 bottom: Photo © Ami Vitale
p.87: Photo © Curtis Cowgill
p.88 left: Photo provided by Fred Bercovitch
p.88 right: Photo © Slawek K on Unsplash
p.89: Photo © Gwen Weustink on Unsplash
p.90/91: Photo © worldswildlifewonders on Shutterstock
p.92: Photo © Volodymyr Burdiak on Shutterstock
p.93: Photo © Luke Shelley on Shutterstock
p.94: Photo © Creel on Shutterstock
p.95: Photo © Kitch Bain on Shutterstock

p.96: Photo © Charles-Alexandre Plaisir
p. 97: Photo © Ethan Brooke on Unsplash
p.99: Photo © David Clode on Unsplash
p.100: Photo © Benny Marty on Shutterstock
p.101 right–p.104: Photos © Geoff Shaw
p.105: Photo © Kellie Leigh, Science for Wildlife
p.107–p.109: Photos © Uli Kunz; Instagram @uli_kunz
p.110/111: Photo © Sebastian Pena Lambarri on Unsplash
p.112: Photo © Jeremy Bishop on Unsplash
p.113: Photo © Isai Dominguez Guerrero
p.114 top: Photo © Jackie Ziegler
p.114 bottom: Photo provided by Jackie Ziegler
p.115: Photo © Jodi Frediani
p.116 and p.118: Photo © Giverny Forbes
p.119: Photo © Andy Thompson
p.120: Photo © Giverny Forbes
p.121: Photo © Andy Thompson
p.122 left: Photo © Jason Zhao on Unsplash
p.122 right and p.123: Photos © Lazlo Peter
p.125, p.126, p.128, p.131, p.132 (large), p.133: Photos © Isai Dominguez Guerrero
p.129 and p.130 left: Photo © Natalie Davis
p. 132 bottom left: Photo © Harvey Lemelin
p. 132 top right: Photo © Elaine Wiersma Mariposa
p.139: Photo © Bob Brewer on Unsplash
p.140 top: Photo © Chris Charles on Unsplash
p.144 bottom: Photo provided by Raquel Costa
p.149 top: Photo © Uli Kunz; Instagram @uli_kunz
p.149 2nd from top: Photo © Jodi Frediani
p.149 3rd from top: Photo © Shaun Templeton
p.149 bottom: Photo © Shaun Templeton
p.154: Photo © Martina Sandkühler

Index

Bold page numbers indicate
  photographs.

A

Africa 25, 76, 80, 84, 135, 139, 140: *see
  also* Botswana, Congo, Kenya, South
  Africa, Tanzania, Uganda
Alaska (USA) **42–3**
Amboseli National Park (Kenya) **78–9**,
  86–7
Antarctic Research Trust (ART) 28
Antarctica **23**, **24**, 29, **33**, 150–1: tourism
  150–1
Apes, Great 134–45: appeal 135; and
  humans 135; images **134–45**;
  intelligence 135; language 135, 138;
  reproduction 138; social behaviour
  135; tool use 135; *see also* individual
  ape entries
appeal (of wildlife) 10, 16, 22, 27, 29, 30,
  34, 39, 46, 48, 52–3, 62, 65, 68, 72, 74,
  84, 88, 90, 93–4, 96, 98, 102, 104–5,
  114–15, 117, 123, 124, 133, 135, 144
Arctic Ocean 42, 45
Argentina 25
Asia 68, 76, 111, 135, 139
Audley, Katherina **20**, 20–1
Australia 25, 90, 94, 96–7, 98, 102, **108**,
  151

B

baby schema (*Kindchenschema*) 10
backyards, urban (New Zealand) 12–13
Bauer, Thomas 150–1
Bear, Brown/Grizzly **40**, 41, **42–4**: cubs
  42–4; female with cubs **42–3**; fishing
  40
Bear, Panda **38–9**
Bear, Polar 9, 41, **41**, 42, 45, **45**, 46,
  46, 47, **47**: appeal 46; colouration
  42; cubs 45, **47**; female with cub

47; fur 42; and global warming 42,
  45; marine mammal 42; paws 45;
  reproduction 45; and sea ice 42, 45;
  sense of smell 42, 45; and tourism
  45, 46
bears 38–47: appeal 39
behaviour, human 9
Bercovitch, Fred 88, **88**, 89
biodiversity 12–13, 72, 89, 90, 94, 155
biophilia 12–13, 149: Biophilia Theory 12
birdfeeders 123
Bonobos 135
Borneo 140
Botswana **66**, **68**, **76–7**, **83**
Bueddefeld, Jill 46, **46**, 47
Butterfly, Monarch 124–33: appeal
  124, 133; colouration 124; diet 124,
  129; images **124–33**; life cycle 129;
  migration 124, 129, 132–3; milkweed
  129, **129**, **130**, 132; in oyamel fir trees
  124–8, **131**, **132**; pattern **129**; pupa
  130; tourism 132, **132**, 133; toxicity
  124, 129
Bwindi Impenetrable National Park
  (Uganda) **136–7**, 140, **142–3,** 144–5

C

California (USA) 53, 61, 129
Canada 33, 46, **46**, 47, 129, 130, 132
Cape Kidnappers (Hawke's Bay, New
  Zealand) 129
Cape Otway (Victoria, Australia) 102
Cape Town (South Africa) **62**
cassowaries 151
Cats, Big 64–73: appeal 65, 68; and
  genetic tools 72–3; as pets 65
charismatic creatures 10
Cheetah **66**, 68–9, **69**: cubs 68, **69**;
  family **66**; mother and cubs **69**; speed
  68
children 12–13: social environments 13

Chile 25
Chimpanzees **134–5**, 138, **138**, 140,
  140, **148**: and tourism **148**
China **38–9**, 39
chlamydia 101–2
Christmas Island (Australia) **108**
Churchill (Manitoba, Canada) 46, **46**, 47
citizen science projects 20
climate change 29, 42, 46–7, 97, 105,
  110, 149
Coca-Cola (and Polar Bears) 47
Colobus, Red 140
communication, conservation/science
  47, 149, 152, 154–5
Congo, Democratic Republic of 140
connection with nature 12, 21, 47, 62–3,
  73, 152
conservation: and marketing 154–5; and
  relationships 155
conservation programs/projects 9,
  12–13, 20–1, 28–9, 36–7, 46–7, 52–3,
  60–3, 72–3, 80–3, 88–9, 96–7, 104–5,
  114–15, 122–3, 132–3, 144–5, 150–1,
  154–5
conservation, strategies of hope for 13,
  21, 29, 37, 47, 53, 62–3, 73, 82, 89, 97,
  105, 115, 123, 133, 145, 151, 155
Costa, Raquel 144, **144**, 145
Cousteau, Jacques 54
cuteness 10

D

Davis, Lloyd Spencer 98
Davis, Scott 2, 61, **61**, 62–3
dingo 94, 97
disconnect, urban 12, 46
Dominica **14–15**, **146–7**
Dominican Republic **19**
Dunedin (New Zealand) 123

E

echolocation 14
ecosystem, care for 12, 105, 115
ecotourism, marine 114–15
Elephant Sanctuary, Reteti (Kenya) **80**,
  80–3
Elephant, African 5, 74–83: appeal 74;
  drinking **74–5**, **81**, **83**; forest and
  savannah subspecies 74; herd **78–9**,
  83; images **74–9**, **81**, **83**; intelligence
  77; ivory poaching 74, 76; matriarch
  and family **76–7**; mother and young
  81; reproduction 76; social animal 77;
  trunk 76; young playing **76**
Elephant, Asian 74, 76
elephants 74–83
environmental sustainability 151
eucalyptus **100–1**, 101, 102, **103**, 104,
  105

F

Falkland Islands **27**, 28, **28**, 29, **34**
Felton (California, USA): forest **13**
Festa-Bianchet, Marco **96**, 96–7
Finkler, Wiebke 2, **154**, 154–5
flagship species 9
flax, New Zealand **118**
Franz Josef Land (Russia) **45**

G

Galápagos Islands (Ecuador) 25
Gannet, Australasian 129
gardens 12–13
Geijer, Christina **80**, 80–2
giraffes 84–9: appeal 84; calves 84; eyes/
  eyelashes **89**; feet 86; group **84–5**;
  height 84; images **84–9**; neck 84, 88;
  as pollinators 86; reproduction 86–7;
  Reticulated **87**; skin patterns 84; teeth
  86; tongue 86, **88**
global warming 27, 42, 45:

see also climate change
Goodall, Jane 5
Gorillas 140, 144–5: appeal 144; baby **142–3**; behaviour 144; eyes **141**; mother and baby **145**; Mountain Gorilla **136–7**, 140, **141**, 144, **144**, 145; silverback **144**; silverback and family **136–7**; tourism 140, 144–5
Gorillas in the Mist 145
Grizzly *see* Brown Bear
Guadalupe Island, Mexico **54–5**, **57–61**, **148**
Guerrero, Mexico 20–1, **20–1**

H
Happy Whale initiative 19
Hoiho/Yellow-eyed Penguin 24, **25**, 148, **149**: nesting 25; reproduction 148, tourism 25, 149
Holbox, Mexico **114**
hope 9–10, 154–5: hope-based science 155; Hope Theory 9; science of 9
hopelessness 152
human behaviour 82
human–wildlife encounters 36; *see also* tourism
Hungary **11**
Hynes, Emily **104**, 104–5

I
Indigenous people, North American 133
International Union for the Conservation of Nature 48, 58, 102

J
Jaws 54

K
Kākā 116–23: appeal 117, 123; chicks 121; colouration **117**, **121**; conservation ambassadors 122–3;

diet 118; feeding **118**, **122**; images **117–23**; leg band **120–1**; and Māori 117, 123; mōkai rangatira 123; monitoring **120–1**, 123; predators 118, 121; reproduction 118, 121; sanctuaries 121, 123; talons **119**
Kangaroo, Eastern Grey 94, **94–6**, 96–7, **97**: joey in pouch **95**; mother and joey 94, **97**; reproduction 96–7
Kangaroo, Red 90, **91–2**, 93, **93**: blue fliers 91: mother and joey **91–2**; relaxing **92–3**
Kangaroo, Western Grey 94
kangaroos 90–7: appeal 90, 93–4, 96; defence 93; joeys 90, **91–2**, 93, **94**, **95**, **97**; management 94; monitoring 96; movement 93; pouch 90, 93, 94, **95**; reproduction 93, 94, 96
kangaroos, sthenurine 93
kangaroos, tree 90
Kenya **64–5**, **69**, **74–6**, **78–9**, 80, **80**, **81**, 82–3, **86–7**
Kenya Wildlife Service 80
keystone species 48, 53
King Kong 145
Koala 98–105: appeal 98, 102, 104–5; and chlamydia 101–2; claws **101**; contraception 104–5; diet 101; and eucalyptus **100–1**, 101, 102, **103**, 104, **105**; images **98–104**; joey 101, **102**; management 104–5; mother and joey **102**; pap 101–2; pouch 101; reproduction 101

L
ladybird **11**
Lake Nakuru (Kenya) **64–5**
Last Child in the Woods 12
Lemelin, Harvey **132**, 132–3
Leopard, Snow 68, 71, **71**, 72–3, **73**: appeal 72; fur 71, **71**; jumping ability

71; monitoring 72; tail 71
Lion, African **64–5**, 64–7, **67**, 68, **68**, **70**: communication 66–7; cub **68**, **70**; diet 66; females **64–5**; male **67**, **70**; male with cub **70**; mane 66; pride 66
Lorenz, Konrad 10
Louv, Richard 12
Lowekutuk, Dorothy 80, **80**
Lower Mustang (Nepal) **72**

M
Mackenzie, Tahu 122, **122**, 123, **123**
Mackerel **57**, **60–1**
Maldives **110–11**
Māori 117, 123
marine management and protection plans 20
marketing and conservation 154–5
marsupials 90, 98
Masai Mara (Kenya) **69**
Medawar, Sir Peter 88
megafauna 14, 46, 47
Mexico 20–1, **20–1**, **54–5**, **57–61**, **114**, **124–8**, 129, 130, **130–1**, 132–3, **132–3**, **148**
Micronesia **153**
milkweed 129, 132
Mission Beach (Queensland, Australia) 151
Monarch Butterfly Biosphere Reserve (Mexico) 130
Monterey Bay (California, USA) **18**, **51**, **149**

N
Namunyak Wildlife Conservancy, Kenya 80
National Geographic channel 46
nature deficit disorder 12
Nepal **72**
New Zealand **8**, 12–13, 25, **25**, **36**, 117,

118, 121, 122–3, **123**, 148, **149**
Norway **32**, **35**, **41**, **47**, **151**

O
Orangutans **139**, 140: female **139**; mother and baby **140**; reproduction 140
Orca/Killer Whale 14, **17**, 57–8
Oregon (USA) 53
Orokonui Ecosanctuary (New Zealand) 122–3, **123**
Otago Peninsula (New Zealand) 25, **149**
oyamel fir trees **124–8**, **131–3**

P
pademelons 90
Pagel, Chantal **36**, 36–7
palm oil 140
Panda, Giant 9, **38–9**, 39, 40: appeal 39
Pannonhalma (Hungary) **11**
parrots 117
Penguin, African 25
Penguin, Emperor 22, 24, **24**, **27**, **151**: chicks **23**, 24, **24**, **25**, **27**; egg incubation 24; feather density 24; grooming **27**
Penguin, Galápagos 25
Penguin, Humboldt 25
Penguin, King 24–5, **26**, **27**, 28–9, 150: chicks 24, 25, **25**; monitoring 28
Penguin, Little 25
Penguin, Magellanic 25
Penguin, Southern Rockhopper 28, **28**, 29, **29**, **150–1**: colony **28**, **150**; crest **29**; monitoring 28; tagging **28**
Penguin, Yellow-eyed/Hoiho 24, **25**, 148, **149**: adult with chick **149**; nesting 25; reproduction 148; tourism 25, 149, **149**
penguins 22–9, 148–51: adaptations to aquatic lifestyle 22, 24, 29; appeal 22,

27, 29; egg incubation 24; monitoring 28; wings 22
Peru 25
Phillip Island (Victoria, Australia) 25
photography, online wildlife 37
Polar Bear Alex 46
possums, brushtail 118, 121
Project Antarctic Conservation 151
Puijila (fossil seal) 33
Pütz, Klemens **28**, 28–9
pyramids, ancient Mexican 132–3

R
rainforests, tropical 140
rats 118, 121
Reteti Elephant Sanctuary (Kenya) **80**, 80–3
Rowe, Katie 80, **80**

S
Samburu community (Kenya) 80, 82
Samburu National Park (Kenya) **76**, **81**
Schmitt, Natalie 72, **72**, 73
science communication 149, 152, 154, 155
Scott Polar Research Institute (Cambridge University) 151
Seadragon **149**
sea ice 42, 45
Sea Lion 33, 58
Sea Otter Awareness Week 53
Sea Otter, Southern (California Sea Otter) 48–9, **48–9**, 50, **50**, 51, **51**, 52–3, **53**: appeal 48, 52–3; aquatic life 48, 51; behaviour 52–3; diet 52; ecosystem role 52–3; feeding 51, **51**; fur 51; grooming **50**, 51; juvenile **53**; and kelp forests 48; keystone species 48, 53; mother and pup **51**; pups 51, **51**, 52, 53; rafts 51; tool use 51, 52; webbed hind feet **53**

Seal, Crabeater 33
Seal, Elephant (Southern) **31**, 33, 34, **34**, 58: male and female **34**; weight 33
Seal, Harp 33, 34
Seal, Leopard 33, **33**
Seal, Southern Fur **37**
Seal, Weddell 33
seals and sea lions 30–7: ancestry 30; appeal 30, 34; blubber 33; clubbing 34; diet 33; Otariid family/'eared' 33; pelts 34; Phocid family 33; pups 34; reproduction 33; tourism 36–7
Seddon, Philip 146
selfies, wildlife 36, 37, 146–9
Serengeti National Park (Tanzania) **84–5**
shark products 111
Shark, Great White 54–63: appeal 58, 62; breaching attack **63**; in California 60–3; colouration 57; images **54–63**, **148**; monitoring 61; as predator 57, **63**; reproduction 57; warm-bloodedness 57
Shark, Whale 106–15: appeal 114–15; diet 106, 109; filter feeding 106, 109, **113**; images 7, **106–15**; and remora fish **112**; reproduction 109; skin 111; skin pattern 109; solitary 111; tourism 111, **114**, **115**, **148**
Sierra Madres (Mexico) 133
Snyder, Charles R. 9
social media 36, 37, 148, 149, 154
South Africa 25, **56**, **62**, **63**
South Georgia Island **25**, **26**, **31**, **37**, 151
Spencer Davis, Lloyd 22
Squid, Giant 16
Staedler, Michelle 52, **52–3**
stoats 118, 121
storytelling 154–5
Sumatra 140
Svalbard (Norway) **32**, **35**, **41**, **47**, **151**

T
Tanzania **84–5**
Tararua Range forest (New Zealand) **8**
Tiger 65: in captivity 65
Tonga, Kingdom of **18**, **20**
tourism, wildlife 16, 19, 25, 36–7, 45, 47, 111, **114**, 114–15, **115**, 132–3, 140, 144–5, 149, 150–1: sustainable 146–9; wildlife viewing practices 148–9
turtles, sea **153**

U
Uganda **134–8**, 140, **140**, **142–3**, 144–5, **145**
United States **13**, **18**, **42–3**, **51**, 52–3, 61, 65, 129, 130, 132, **149**
urchins, sea 48, 53

V
Van Heezik, Yolanda 12, **12**, 13
Virunga (Democratic Republic of Congo) 140

W
wallabies 90
Wallaroo, Common 94
Walrus **32**, 33, **35**
whale watching 16, 19
Whale, Blue: size 16
Whale, Humpback 16, **16**, 17, **18**, **19**, 20–1: baleen **16**; calves **18**, **19**, **20**, 21; feeding **16**; songs 16; and tourism **149**, **150**; visual displays 16, 21
Whale, Killer/Orca 14, **17**, 57–8: female **17**
Whale, Sperm **14–15**, 16, **146–7**: markings 16
whales 9, 14–21, **146–7**: appeal 16; baleen 14, 16, **16**; communication 16, 21; intelligence 16, markings 19, monitoring 19; songs 16, toothed 14,

16; tourism 16, 19
Whales of Guerrero 20–1, **20–1**
wildlife tourism *see* tourism
Williams, Betty 10
wombat 98
World Wildlife Fund 39

Y
Yellow-eyed Penguin/Hoiho 148, **149**: reproduction 148; tourism 149

Z
Zambia **67**
Ziegler, Jackie **114**, 114–15

ACKNOWLEDGEMENTS

This book would not have been possible without the support of many people. Firstly, the wonderful team at Exisle Publishing: Gareth St John Thomas, Anouska Jones, Karen Gee and Mark Thacker. Thank you for your expertise, support and patience along this journey. To my collaborator Scott Davis — thank you for your photographic genius and for simply being a nice human to work with despite a very busy schedule. A big thank you goes to all the story contributors as well as chapter co-authors — your expertise, insights and trust greatly influenced the publication. And finally, this project would not have been possible without the love and support of my family: my partner Lloyd for giving me the necessary space, inspiration and reminders when I couldn't see the light at the end of the tunnel. To my sons Lewis, Milos and Eligh — thank you for reminding me every day of what matters most and still letting Mum do 'her thing'. To my own Mum and my late Dad — you offered me a backyard filled with trees when I needed it most. No words can express my gratitude for all you have done for this *Menschenjunges*. To Markus, Oliver, Domenic, Kelsey and Daniel — you are an important part of My Whole. And finally, thank you life — I'm humbled beyond words for the ride.

First published 2021

Exisle Publishing Pty Ltd

226 High Street, Dunedin, 9016, New Zealand

PO Box 864, Chatswood, NSW 2057, Australia

www.exislepublishing.com

Copyright © 2021 in text: Wiebke Finkler.

Copyright © 2021 in images: Scott Davis, with the exception of those listed in the photographic credits on p. 156.

Wiebke Finkler and Scott Davis assert the moral right to be identified as the creators of this work.

A CiP record for this book is available from the National Library of Australia.

ISBN 978-1-925820-64-5

Designed by Mark Thacker

Typeset in Myriad Pro 10 on 15pt

Printed in China

This book uses paper sourced under ISO 14001 guidelines from well-managed forests and other controlled sources.

10 9 8 7 6 5 4 3 2 1

Disclaimer

While this book is intended as a general information resource and all care has been taken in compiling the contents, neither the author nor the publisher and their distributors can be held responsible for any loss, claim or action that may arise from reliance on the information contained in this book.